REVISITING THE SCENE OF WRITING: NEW READINGS OF CIXOUS

Edited by Julia Dobson and Gill Rye

Contents

Introduction JULIA DOBSON AND GILL RYE	243
Hélène Cixous's *A True Garden*: An Introduction CLAUDINE G. FISHER	248
A True Garden by Hélène Cixous Translated by CLAUDINE G. FISHER	252
Identification and Melancholia: The Inner Cinema of Hélène Cixous EMMA WILSON	258
At the Time of Writing Theatre: Cixous's Absolute Present JULIA DOBSON	270
Of Altobiography MAIREAD HANRAHAN	282
Agony or Ecstasy? Reading Cixous's Recent Fiction GILL RYE	296
The Ethics of Rewriting the Loss of Exile in *Manne aux Mandelstams aux Mandelas* SARAH COOPER	311

Millennial Fears: Fear, Hope and Transformation
in Contemporary Feminist Writing   324
MORAG SHIACH

An Interview with Hélène Cixous   338
IAN BLYTH

Hélène Cixous, *Tambours sur la digue*, performed by
the Théâtre du Soleil, Paris, May 2000: A First Response   344
JULIA DOBSON

Hélène Cixous – A Selected Bibliography   350

Claudine Fisher's translation appears with the permission of Editions
des femmes: *Un vrai jardin* by Hélène Cixous (new edition)
(c) 1998, Des femmes,
6, rue de Mézières, 75006 Paris, France
All rights reserved.

Introduction

This issue of *Paragraph*, 'Revisiting the Scene of Writing: New Readings of Cixous', aims both to reflect and to foster the extraordinary ongoing impact of Hélène Cixous's writing across a wide spectrum of academic disciplines and literary forms. The influence of Cixous's prolific and rich oeuvre continues to be felt on an international scale more than thirty years after her first works were published. The contributions to this volume 'revisit' Cixous's texts from the entire extent of her corpus, from Claudine Fisher's translation of and introduction to the poetical short story, *Un vrai jardin* (*A True Garden*) (1971), to Julia Dobson's response to the latest offering for the stage, *Tambours sur la digue* (2000), and they take in the full range of her literary production which comprises essays, fiction, plays, short stories, poetical meditations, readings of literature and art, and autobiographical writing.

It is clear then that the full diversity of Cixous's writing does not fail to stimulate critical interest, yet her profile within the realms of anglophone literary academia is, to a great extent, still dominated by her seminal, theoretical works of the 1970s, which introduced the concept of *écriture féminine* and established the radical, liberating and provocative project of 'writing the body'. Her own body of fictional and theatrical work, for which she is best known in France, remains only selectively read or taught. *La Jeune Née* (*The Newly Born Woman*) has remained on reading lists for French women's writing courses, yet her fictions of the last ten years have not found a place in studies of contemporary writing in France. Moreover, Cixous's status as a major playwright in France, which, by means of her collaboration with Mnouchkine's Théâtre du Soleil, also forms one of the most influential partnerships in contemporary French theatre, has not yet been reflected either in academic programmes or in critical receptions of her work internationally. By revisiting the scenes of Cixous's writing, this collection of essays points to the wider engagement with the full range of her oeuvre that is currently being undertaken in fields as diverse as art history, archaeology, philosophy and translation studies and aims to generate a greater interest in Cixous's more recent fictions and theatre.

Both Cixous's work itself and readings of it have often met with accusations of elitism and utopianism. It is hoped that this volume, whilst celebrating the undoubtedly 'difficult joys' of Cixous's work, also establishes a critical space in which other voices can be heard. The contributors to this issue of *Paragraph* include both established specialists and new researchers in Cixous studies. They all offer fresh perspectives on, and a critical engagement with, Cixous's texts. The essays demonstrate a wide range of approaches to Cixous's writing, but they all address, in different ways, one of the most common threads of her work: the relation between self and other. This theme remains a constant Cixousian concern, whether it is approached from the perspective of loss (in particular, the death of Cixous's father which permeates her whole oeuvre), gender, love, politics, or writing itself. It is this unswerving attention to the complexity of the dynamics of human relations which endows Cixous's writing with its universal dimension and which renders her texts worth revisiting again and again.

One of the reasons for the imbalance in the reception of Cixous's work internationally has been the problems her polyphonic, poetical writing presents to translators. In the new interview, with Ian Blyth, that appears in this volume, Cixous herself speaks of the difficulty her translators have with rendering into other languages the richness of the linguistic play which characterizes her writing. For this reason, throughout this volume, all quotations from Cixous's work are given in both French and English. Published translations are used wherever possible; elsewhere, unless otherwise stated, the translations are the contributor's own. A new translation revisits the original scene of writing in the most explicit sense, and it is with Claudine Fisher's hitherto unpublished translation of one of Cixous's earliest texts, *Un vrai jardin*, that this volume opens. Fisher's introduction to the translation shows how this poetical short story serves as a clear demonstration of both the continuity and development of the major concerns of Cixous's work. The text, written in 1971 and re-published by Editions des femmes in 1998, engages with constructs of sexual and collective identities, borders and belonging, absence and loss, questions which power Cixous's writing and which constitute recurrent themes throughout her oeuvre.

Indeed, it is the representation of loss that is central to Emma Wilson's exploration of the status of the visual within the dynamics of identification in Cixous's texts, a response which she sets in the context of her own personal revisiting of Cixous. Revealing an 'inner cinema' which enables a revision of scopic economies and posits a more positive relationship between self and image, yet admits ultimately the powerful absence inherent in its structure, Wilson's article suggests examples of cinematic practice that might carry some of the traits of this 'inner cinema', before returning to assert the radical implications of Cixous's practice for cultural discourses of mourning and memory. The imperative in Cixous's texts of recognizing and inscribing the complex relationships between loss, desire and memory are further discussed in Julia Dobson's article on the temporal implications in Cixous's aesthetics of writing for the theatre. The potential tension between the role of writing as inscription of ethical, political and personal engagements and writing as an open-ended and fragile process is identified in both Cixous's writing on the theatre and her recent plays. The article tracks Cixous's search for a temporal site in which past and present can fruitfully coexist in the theatre and suggests that the time of writing itself provides a solution in Cixous's most recent plays.

Cixous's writing on the theatre has repeatedly claimed the form as a utopian site for the rethinking and re-presentation of the relationship between self and other, writer and text, actor and spectator, author and reader. However, in her writing more generally, such specificities are rare, and her own fictions resist generic categorization, often evoking events from her own life: the plurilingualism of her childhood environment, the double 'exile' of one perceived by Algerians as French and by the French as Jewish in Algeria, her father's death and her status on arriving in France as 'juifemme' (jewoman). What, as Mairead Hanrahan asks in her essay in this volume, are the consequences of such autobiographical presences in Cixous's work? Hanrahan's study, which introduces the new term of 'altobiography', forms a response to questions of the role of autobiography and theories of the autobiographical in Cixous's fictions. An engagement with Cixous's apparent rejection of autobiography leads, through a close textual reading of passages from *Hélène Cixous, Photos de racines* (*Hélène Cixous, Rootprints*), to a model of writing as re-rooting, of narrative as self-discovery. How does this particular relationship between writing self and narrative impact upon the reader's encounter with Cixous's texts? This is one of the questions asked in Gill Rye's article which takes as its starting point the often polarized response to reading Cixous. Exploring the effects, both seductive and alienating, on the reader of such Cixousian strategies as direct address, self-referentiality, intertextuality and poetic play, Rye's closing discussion of *Beethoven à jamais ou l'existence de Dieu* endows the textual space with a potentially transformative impact on the reader through the process of reading.

Since the early 1980s, many commentators have perceived a shift in Cixous's writing and this has been differently represented as a movement from the personal to the historical, from self to other, from inner drama to world stage. Whilst such generalizations might be seen as ultimately reductive, the question of the representation of the other is central to such changes in scale. Cixous's plays and fictions have been set within the partition of India, the bitter struggles for political control of Cambodia, the impact of Stalin's regime on poetry and cultural memory, corruption and negligence within the political and medical establishments of contemporary France and the imprisoned existence of Nelson Mandela and Osip Mandelshtam. Cixous has written extensively about the journey she makes as a writer to inhabit or to portray the other and her preferred form for such 'démoïsations' (a Cixousian neologism denoting both dispossession and harvest) remains the theatre. In her discussion of *Manne aux Mandelstams aux Mandelas*, Sarah Cooper considers the ethical implications of treading a narrative tightrope that aims to enable the bearing of witness to the pain or death of others without submerging their voices. Tracing the development of Cixous's aesthetics of alterity from her early writings on *écriture féminine* to her descriptions of writing for the theatre that encompass differences other than sexual difference, Cooper suggests that the loss of authorial self may offer conflicting tropes of self-sacrifice and colonization that undermine Cixous's presentation of the position of the other in this text.

The political thrust of Cixous's work, which, despite its controversial reception, has been so influential on feminist issues, lies in the ways in which it enables different ways of thinking. The relationship between Cixous's oeuvre and contemporary feminisms is addressed provocatively by Morag Shiach in her mapping of the coexistence of fear and hope in selected works of Hélène Cixous, Seyla Benhabib and Sadie Plant. Shiach's quest for representations of hope is set in the context of Ulrich Beck's work on the political consequences of contemporary millennial discourses of fear and risk in their erosion of utopianism and dismissal of hope for change. Shiach reads the texts discussed as maintaining a struggle central to all feminist projects: the insistence on finding new modes of thinking and imagining which counter fear of change and loss. Thus, she places Cixous's recent fictions in a new and exciting context.

The final two pieces in this volume constitute engagements with very recent manifestations of Cixous's work. Ian Blyth's interview with Cixous, conducted in June 1999, animates and develops many of the themes that permeate this volume; the relationship between identity, writing and exile, the desire to 'write the present' and the relationship between self and narrative. The interview reflects Cixous's ceaseless investigation of her own writing practices and as such is central to her writing on writing. Julia Dobson's response to Cixous's latest play, in production at the Cartoucherie from September 1999 until June 2000, serves to remind us further of Cixous's divergent profiles in France and anglophone countries. *Tambours sur la digue* was one of the most popular productions in Paris in 2000 and has garnered several national awards. It indicates the level of success of Cixous's writing for the theatre and confounds interpretations of her plays as merely illustrations of theoretical strategies.

Cixous's writing remains prolific; her latest text at the time of writing this introduction, *Les rêveries de la femme sauvage*, begins with an image of travelling in order not to arrive, of writing an unimaginable text, of losing in order to begin anew. Such persistent enquiry into the personal and public intersections of identity, writing and desire continues to promise as well as to provoke, undoubtedly ensuring future visits to the scenes of Cixous's writing.

JULIA DOBSON
University of Wolverhampton
and
GILL RYE
Institute of Romance Studies (University of London)
and University of Surrey Roehampton

Hélène Cixous's *A True Garden*: An Introduction

Hélène Cixous's *Un vrai jardin* (*A True Garden*) received little attention on its first publication by L'Herne in 1971, although it is a powerful and poetic short story.[1] Re-published by Editions des femmes in 1998, the text deserves a more notable place in Cixous's prolific output; the movement from body to history, from birth to writing, from subject to alterity, that is figured within it, foreshadows many of her later works. As one of Cixous's earliest fiction texts, this poetic piece also re-works both themes and motifs already found in her first works, *Prénom de Dieu*, which foregrounds questions of origin and identity, *Dedans* (*Inside*), where the tension between inside and outside is at play, *Le Troisième Corps* and *Les Commencements*, both of which are concerned with absence, death and love.[2] Dedicated to the writer's maternal grandmother, Omi, *A True Garden* addresses the theme of loss, on personal, metaphorical and conceptual levels. Loss is perceived through the eyes of a child who is looking for both his origins and an identity, but this story gradually becomes a reflection of life in modern times. The tone of the piece retains a constant sobriety yet Cixous's poetic language is given full rein.

Unusually in Cixous's work, the question of identity is approached from the perspective of a little boy, the masculine voice both corresponding to the grammatical masculine gender with which the child is addressed by two groups of adults (guards and nursemaids) and enabling the fusion of the child with the garden (also a masculine noun in French) at the end of the story. The reader wonders whether it is the garden or the child who is talking; an effect of suspense is thus created, while, at the same time, the final merging of the two is being prepared. Such deliberate blurring is especially significant since, either considered as 'that' or called 'filth' by the adults, the child with no name is in the process of pondering his nameless nature. The relationship between naming and identity that is foregrounded here remains a constant feature throughout Cixous's work. Later on, she will continue to explore in depth the problems of the patronymic and naming of the Other.[3]

The tensions between lived reality and the symbolic meaning of the law, which come into their own in Cixous's feminist essays of the 1970s, such as 'Le Rire de la Méduse' ('The Laugh of the Medusa'), as well as in later fiction, such as *Limonade tout était si infini* , can already be seen surfacing in this text through the different roles of the adults who are present and the father who is absent.[4] Cixous deconstructs the symbolic positioning of the adults by showing that the guards represent the law in all its shortcomings. Their overseeing functions prove their 'under seeing' in reality. Similarly, the nursemaids, (ironical 'good women', *les bonnes*) represent a false version of motherhood. Rather, they are mother-surrogates, their thighs and black-stockings arousing the child's curiosity and transmitting a sexual message which he only half perceives. He receives neither support nor guidance from these adults, and this lack is at the heart of his alienation.

The theme of the absent father permeates all Cixous's work, and here, it brings about a move away from reality in order to access the dream world of the child. Paradoxically, the non-existence of the father actually inscribes his very presence in the text. The child's sheer desire of, and belief in, the possibility of the father's presence renders it tangible, although the child himself recognizes that he (the father) is really only a metaphor. Yet, despite his lucidity, the child wishes to believe in his own illusion: perhaps the father will come, since he wishes him to. The child's quandary is extremely moving and serves to underline the hopelessness of his plight all the more. As expected Saviour, the father is ultimately the figure of destruction, finally arriving in the form of a bomb, a symbol of law taken to the extreme. Throughout her writing, Cixous has given the father a privileged place both as source of feelings of loss or exile, and at the same time, as proof of the existence of the Other and source of inspiration. The symbolic father permits the existence of all metamorphoses: his presence within can transform absence and silence into life.

In *A True Garden*, alienation and exile, partly embodied in the absent father, are reinforced by means of the inside/outside opposition. The primitive scene evoked by this story symbolizes the original absence of the father which pushes the child 'outside' into the world. As soon as the child discovers the garden and passes through the gate, he is once again 'inside'. Within the prison-like railings and even though he has been forced 'outside', the child experiences freedom. He escapes from the outside world which was in fact the real prison, and he is now able to dream. This paradox is one of Cixous's recurrent motifs and will be expanded into her theoretical praxis. Appearing in her early fiction, it is often revisited, for example, in 'My Algeriance, in other words: to depart not to arrive from Algeria' almost thirty years later. In this essay, Cixous returns to her own first memory of alienation, when her Jewish family were expelled from the Military Circle in Oran.[5] The quota which was imposed on admittance to the Circle brings about exclusion at the very instant that it allows inclusion. In *A True Garden*, it is only when the child moves from the 'outside' of the home that he experiences the 'inside' of the garden and recognizes the simple act of being and existing. Alienation and exile always function in close relationship to the search for origins and to the possibility of a beyond. The 'coming' (*venue*) of the father in *A True Garden* already carries the double significance of 'coming' and 'giving birth' which will appear in many future Cixousian texts. If the father has a role to play in the quest for identity, so too does the mother figure. At first, since the adults encountered in the garden are inadequate representatives, the discovery of a meaning to his existence eludes the child. However, at the moment when he falls 'inside' a maid's thighs in a mock return to the womb, he perceives a suggestion of his origins. At the threshold of life, he becomes aware of marginality. He is then free to be 'outside' in order to become more truly Other. In later works also, Cixous will link inside/outside and belonging/exile themes to birth in all its forms, in order to illustrate issues such as the movement towards the Other, feminine consciousness, coming to writing.

In *A True Garden*, we can perhaps already identify the mark of Cixous's future concept, 'writing the body'. Here, parts of the body and their functions acquire special significance. In literal as well as figurative terms, the child's navel is both the tangible proof of birth and the unavoidable signature of death. At the end of the dream vision, the bomb explodes precisely on his navel, in a powerful personal and universal destruction. In addition to this first set of metaphors of the body, a second set of physical and sensory tropes adds to the poetic dimension of the text. Cixous extends the parameters of touch and gaze not only to express the physicality of the child but also to underscore the dream-like qualities of the garden. The child's very voice and gaze, his love for the garden and the wonders of his imagination are proof of his existence. It is then that the symbiosis of the child with the earth fully occurs. The only true return to the womb is accomplished through a unity with the garden, earth and sand. When the child is at one with the garden his best instincts are brought forth; gentleness, understanding and love accompany his newly acquired inward growth. The bomb explodes when the child 'sees'. It is the child, apparently near-sighted, who can see the truth of the inner nature of the garden and of himself. His selective myopia leads him to true discovery.

In its concern with universal themes of truth and hope, life and death, presence and absence, *A True Garden* stands out within the body of Cixous's early work, meriting more detailed analysis than has hitherto been forthcoming. The child's short-sightedness allows him to see beyond the realm of the law and to concentrate all his imagination and sensitivity into creativity. The grains of sand he holds in his hand, which are not relinquished, even at the height of suffering and absence, reflect grand Cixousian themes of multiplicity and love. Thus the poetic undertones of *A True Garden* highlight the hopes of finding, within the aesthetics of the moment, a symbiosis through creativity. At the same time, this highly poetical short story articulates the song of exile in all human beings.

CLAUDINE G. FISHER
Portland State University

NOTES

1 Hélène Cixous, *Un vrai jardin* (Paris, L'Herne, 1971; re-published des femmes, 1998).
2 *Prénom de Dieu* (Paris, Grasset, 1967); *Dedans* (Paris, Grasset, 1969, re-published des femmes, 1986), *Inside*, translated by Carol Barko (New York, Shocken Books, 1986); *Le Troisième Corps* (Paris, Grasset, 1970); *Les Commencements* (Paris, Grasset, 1970).
3 See Mireille Calle-Gruber and Hélène Cixous, *Hélène Cixous, Photos de racines* (Paris, des femmes, 1994), pp. 84-6, where Cixous discusses the problematic of naming in her texts; Hélène Cixous and Mireille Calle-Gruber, *Hélène Cixous, Rootprints: Memory and Life Writing*, translated by Eric Prenowitz (London and New York, Routledge, 1997), pp.75-8.
4 Hélène Cixous, 'Le Rire de la Méduse', *L'Arc* 61 (1975), 39-54; 'The Laugh of the Medusa', translated by Keith and Paula Cohen, in *New French Feminisms*, edited by Isabelle de Courtivron and Elaine Marks (Brighton, Harvester, 1981), pp. 245-64; Hélène Cixous, *Limonade tout était si infini* (Paris, des femmes, 1982).
5 'My Algeriance, in other words: to depart not to arrive from Algeria', translated by Eric Prenowitz, in *Stigmata, Escaping Texts* (London, New York, Routledge, 1998), pp. 153-72 (p. 159).

A True Garden by Hélène Cixous

To Omi

I entered without mistrust. It was a real garden. From the very garden gate, you could see the earth was there. Then the gate closed softly, and you were inside the garden. Outside and further away, people were going to war. A few bombs would fall, and shake the canvas tent. It hadn't been called sky for some time, because, viewed from here below, it could be seen tearing and fraying away above the walls. The earth smelled good.

I had a name. The town had a name, and everybody had one except the garden, which was called simply the garden because there was only one. Since no one called me, my name eventually became obsolete. For some time, a few years, I pronounced it out loud some days, in case things changed and people started speaking to one another again. In truth, I didn't believe it, but an obscure allegiance still dictated its laws to me. So I never admitted aloud that I was happy to have entered the garden, precisely because it had no name, and that, except for the coleopterans, lepidopters, garden guards, nursemaids and children, I was alone.

I hadn't always been alone; I must have been with someone, maybe even inside someone, since I had a navel in the middle of my belly, visible to the naked eye; but perhaps it wasn't a navel, I was no longer sure from the moment when a nursemaid, walking past, told me that the guards should not leave 'filth' like that lying about, and she had poked the end of her umbrella in the eye of my navel while saying that, and applied small swivelling jerks to my whole body. It had hurt me physically and mentally. Ever since, I'd had a small but throbbing pain in my thing, and above all, an unbearable doubt which eventually contaminated my whole universe from right to left and top to bottom, as well as the fabric of my thoughts across all ages.

As I could no longer remember having been anywhere else, neither what had been outside nor what was behind me at the moment I entered the garden, and, except for the noise of the gate which I could conjure up at will, I heard nothing else behind me, nothing except at times the bombs or the nursemaids. I heard nothing beyond the slight panting of the earth, and I began fearing the worst: in a world where I could be treated in such a way, anything could be expected. I no longer dared to remember that I'd had a name, for fear it would come back to me and would precisely be a name like 'filth' or some other name which would belittle me further. I didn't dare to think either of myself or the nursemaids; I kept recalling the umbrella which opened as it was coming down on me; and I wanted to hide, but I couldn't move fast enough; then it was too late, and I heard the nursemaid. If the umbrella hadn't been there, I could have believed that she was talking about someone else, but it was indeed about me that she had spoken, and I had to listen till the end since it was as though I was nailed to the ground. To add one more detail to the horror of my situation, the nursemaid was standing so that her white volume filled my whole field of vision, and my eyes were full of her milky opacity.

I attribute the worsening of my near-sightedness to this occurrence, but I may be mistaken. I have never been able to see people clearly. My myopia is selective: I can make out to perfection lines, perspectives and objects either in space or isolated, and I have a photographic vision of plants and insects. It is people I see badly, human beings I mean, although I can see the difference between the nursemaids in white, guards in blue, and the mass of children who are smaller than the whites and blues and of brighter and more varied colours.

To come to the point, I started to doubt so miserably that I began to regret having forgotten my name. Then, as I could see less and less, I began thinking of the future. Lastly, as nobody called me, not even 'filth', nothing at all, I began feeling lonely. I started thinking of bombs, of outside, of what must have been behind me when I was at the garden gate. I began wishing and believing. Then praying. Since I knew no prayers, I invented one. It was a simple prayer, and to reinforce it, I would, at times, offer sacrifices, like those I saw the children make: I made a small heap of crickets' legs and butterflies' wings, which I arranged in the shapes of flowers, with the legs for stamens and the wings for petals, and I prayed: 'Come, come, come and get me get me get me, sir, I beg you please come, come.' Once in a while, I sucked on a cricket while praying, and it soothed my impatience. Vanitas. Zero!

One day, a passing guard said to his co-guard (they guarded everything and each other reciprocally): 'Get rid of *that* for me.' It hurt less than for the nursemaid, on the one hand, because it was not the first time that I had experienced contempt, and then, on the other, because I know that guards have a meagre vocabulary. If I actually was 'that', that didn't mean anything, I could be anything. Moreover, I was neither touched nor removed; therefore it may not have been about me.

However, I forced myself, in my innermost self, to recognize the process of regression. In the days of old, I was still on the fringe of the animal realm, now I was driven back into the indefinable. I could have proved my existence and my worth if I had wished; and perhaps I would have done it in person or by writing a protest letter, which tempted me but embarrassed me too, because I didn't know how to undersign; but, in any case, I didn't have to waver for long, since I soon noticed that I wasn't the direct object of disgust but the pretext for a quarrel between two beings who had probably never looked at me. Since they didn't dare to attack each other with their clubs for fear of hurting one another, the guards performed psychological manoeuvres, and I was only a pawn on their chessboard. Every day, they would say: 'Take that away or I'll gobble it up'[1], which frightened me at first but gradually left me cold. Finally, at the onset of indifference, it gave me the idea to take revenge by letting them believe that I'd soon be picked up, which would deprive them of me as intermediary. I had the pleasure of telling them so, straight to their faces, and at last seeing them both look at me. I must point out that I had prepared the offensive for many a long day and each single word was posited and linked to the others in a calculated mixture of irony and offhandedness. I declared: 'Rest assured, sirs, that, from now on, I will guard against presenting myself to you outside your duty hours, for professional reasons, even if they appear to be urgent. Be certain that I will take "that" away myself, and not in any way, would I have allowed myself to linger here, were it not for my father who was supposed to pick me up soon.' If they had begged me to stay, I would have left without hurrying. But they didn't have time, neither did I. A flight of nursemaids all in white rolled in, between them and me, croaking and cackling, chased by a flock of children, sizzling and whistling, who were stoning them. If they had recruited me I would have rejoiced, and picked up the nearest pebbles. But they didn't recognize me. I was about to feel sad, when the two guards began to shout 'Here he is, here he is!' flailing their arms in all directions. In the meantime, my speech had its effect, as much on myself as on them. When I'd told them that my father was going to pick me up, I hadn't believed it. 'Father' was a metaphor. But I'd said it with such rich words that they had taken my statement literally, and they had begun watching not only the garden and each other, but the surroundings as well. By dint of watching, they had ended up believing he was coming. 'Where, from here, no from there, no there, no, here, here, here,' in short, from everywhere. Thus, the rotation of their trunks and arms as well as the vagueness of their information.

Anyhow, they believed they saw him. I felt it was my duty to believe them. I couldn't trust my eyes, since, beyond my outstretched hands, space looked to me like a sheet of still fresh plaster. I was not even sure that it was the nursemaids that I'd heard pass, since I saw only white eggs without faces rolling by, six feet away from me. The guards' conviction mounted. 'Here he is', they screamed. My own conviction became firmer. I was ready. 'I will do my best', I said. Through sheer believing, I began to see, badly but better. 'Your father is waiting for you, hurry up, hurry up', they shouted with confidence. I started running out of caution and obedience, and while I ran I had time to think that, if my father was waiting for me, it wasn't because I'd said he was coming, but rather that I'd said he was coming because I'd foreseen his coming. I ran for a long time because I couldn't see well. But since I was a trusting person, I let myself be guided by instinct. I passed a school of nursemaids. They clapped and said: 'Come on, there he is, you see him, it's him over there, sitting on the slope, it's him!!!' I couldn't see him, but I believed the nursemaids. Moreover, there was a little black on the white.

I reached the slope. Carried away by momentum, hope, belief, fatigue and curiosity, I fell flat on the ground, with open arms and open eyes too. I was lying full length on the slope, which, seen at close range, was not white but ochre. In order to find him, I began to crawl and spread my arms to take in the largest surface possible. I bore him a slight grudge for not coming to meet me, but in turn he must have borne me a grudge for lingering so. I was so busy trying to crawl well that I didn't hear the silence till it ended. Moreover, I took pleasure in feeling the earth rubbing against my belly and my organs.

Eventually I saw the black very near, I jumped on it, with the force of my innocence, each cell of my organism in tune, and I clasped the fat black-hosed knees of an unknown nursemaid. 'I've got him' she cried, opening her thighs, and I fell inside.

Broad laughter shook the earth. They all laughed hard. I felt a sudden sorrow. I so much wanted the nursemaids to cuddle me. I would have done so if I'd been in their place. The one I was under, was laughing so heartily that she was bursting at the seams. She was a fat nursemaid.

I was filled with grief for my own self.

Between the thighs, there was nothing. I believed I saw a white bone, but I no longer believed. Besides, it was all the same to me, I couldn't even complain, I was fine even, and soon after, I was better. Under the knees, I saw the texture of the earth, and I felt I was on familiar ground.

I, too, wanted to laugh in order to do as they did, but laughter didn't come. So, I listened to them all. It was a long laughter. From time to time, there was a bomb, but it was perhaps the laughter of war.

The next day, laughter was still going on. A matter of habit. Rest, Earth, Rest, Earth. Rest. Fewer ideas. No time at all. Except for earth's time. No more emotions except one: I hate nursemaids.

Some entertainment at times such as listening to bombs, looking between the nursemaids' thighs, or better still, when the opportunity arises, stealing a child from them, cutting off one leg before returning him, or forcing a curious little three-year old girl to eat a slug. That makes me laugh.

And one occupation: to ponder my origins, since there is no father for me, or anybody; on the contrary, all against me. Unless my destiny were to be the proof of the existence of the father, but I would know it only at the end.

At the beginning, I didn't know it was the beginning, I had never seen it, I didn't wish to see it. It/he[2] had put me there, a guard had told me, so I was not unaware of it, but this knowledge was only a condensation of words from the mouths of others. In my opinion, the garden and I were linked more closely than the guard and myself. I was even sure, sometimes, that the garden and I were made of the same substance, sand and compost rubbed my bones; moss, fern, violets and strelitzia were growing in my skin, stretching my limbs. In the spring, I let caterpillars crawl up and down on me, in slack and russet processions, and when they made moving rings on my outspread fingers, my skin had the rigidity of bark. I loved sand much more than my own flesh. One day I fell. My hands were filled with sand. I didn't want to let go of it. Madness, the guards could say, when there is so much sand that all the hands of all the men of all the earth would not exhaust it. But I loved it. Does one let go of what one loves because other objects exist? And who would have given me back the same handful? Who would have assured me that I would find again the same sensation of absolute happiness with other grains? Don't we know that happiness is precisely made of the unique conjunction of thousands of irreplaceable grains, held in a single hand, so that we don't know what merges, the hand or the sand? That's why I took care not to lose the happiness I had attained at the end of a long day of trial and error, when I had taken, weighed, shaken, rejected tens of handfuls of sand, not a single one of which had fulfilled me, except precisely the ultimate handful. That's why I fell with a brutal and mineral speed, and went flying to the ground in three places, on the right parietal bone (for I had tried to raise my head), on my elbows pointed forward, my hands tight against my belly, and my knees. On impact, one of my knees, the right, shattered. Lying on the right side, I must have slept for a while, because I remember very well that the sun was on my back at the time my knee gave way, and that, when I saw the sun again, it made, with my left eye, an angle of forty five degrees in relationship to the earth. When I was out, I didn't let go of my sand. I could have done it voluntarily or not, but I never let go when I love. As it was late, I set about standing up. One had to go on living. I looked at myself. I couldn't see myself clearly. I don't see people clearly whereas I perceive the difference in calibre, edges, brightness and weight between two or three grains of sand. I couldn't see myself clearly, but I was used to knowing how to recognize myself through moving and touching. I even saw myself well with my fingers. I had trouble moving. I was tired. I didn't rule out a certain laziness on my part. Lastly, oozing matter was coming out of my knee and I was temporarily sticking to the ground. Blood prevented me from moving and thinking. I spread a little of my sand on it, and the rest, on my leg. The earth smelled good. A few ants were stuck on my leg because of the blood, but were still moving their antennae; I munched on four or five. Four or five bombs fell on the garden by mistake.

All screamed, each one in turn: 'Here they come, here they come!'

The nursemaids were those who ran the fastest. They ran over me so quickly that I didn't even have time to look between their thighs. At that speed all I saw was one enormous thigh with a hundred feet. The guards ran, were ashamed, stopped, and ran again. I felt them pass me, especially those who were looking over their shoulders, and who kicked me sharply on the knee, making the sand fall. Finally everyone had gone but me. One moment later a bomb fell there where I thought my navel was. I exploded. In the past, I would have been frightened. But now I knew that I was the garden. I was the garden. I was inside. I was made of unique diamonds and I had no name. 'Earth, Earth', I cried.

Translated by CLAUDINE G. FISHER
Portland State University

NOTES

1. Play on words of the French expression 'to capture a pawn' at chess or draughts, or jump and remove a piece, literally in slang 'eat it up'.
2. Here Cixous plays on the gender it/he, referring to the beginning, destiny or the father, the father actually becoming one with the beginning.

Identification and Melancholia: The Inner Cinema of Hélène Cixous

Return to Cixous

This will be a study of Cixous, memory and desire. In my own work it marks a return to Cixous: I have largely moved away from writing on literature to work on cinema. Indeed the influence of this shift in my perspective will be felt implicitly and explicitly in this discussion. Coming back to Cixous, I am coming back to the same places in her texts, but knowing them again (as if) for the first time. This is a return to her novel of 1983, *Le Livre de Promethea* (*The Book of Promethea*), and a return to the love between women in Cixous. This is a missing part of my own love story with her texts. It will be a tale of missing the other: a tale of mourning and of failed encounters. This is a belated attempt to understand the place of loss, and what is missing, in the self/other relation in Cixous. In her recent novel *Messie* she writes: 'Histoire sans regret/Mais pas sans manque (…) Il y a du manque, beaucoup de manque./Le manque est à l'intérieur de notre jardin'.[1] (A story without regret/But not without loss (…) There is loss, much loss/Loss is in the interior of our garden). I want here to look at this loss inside.

I have written twice on Cixous before now. My first encounter with her texts is a reading of *Le Livre de Promethea* which I analyse in the context of queer theory.[2] I approach eroticism and sexual identity in Cixous, claiming that in her exploration of each she depends on a refusal of transparency and visibility. Her feminist politics here are seen to be ambiguous. In positive terms, to my mind, Cixous avoids the objectification or fetishization of the female body, while writing about women in love. Yet she avoids political visibility, too, leaving the dissident sexual identity performed in her text both unnamed and unclaimed. Her project entails the destabilization of identity categories in a manner which calls for comparison with the work of Judith Butler; recognition of this underscores my work on Cixous to date. My second encounter with her texts pursues this comparison with Butler, attempting to understand melancholia in Cixous, analysing the ways in which a death, re-narrated, a primary loss, pre-determines the instability of the self in her writing, its dramas of violence and desire.[3] My aim now, in this third encounter, is to re-work these two readings with relation to each other, in order, firstly, to offer a different account of the visual and visibility in Cixous and, secondly, to re-think loss and desire in her work. Here, memory and its dissection in Cixous, will be crucial to both parts of my argument.

Cixous and Vision

Vision, as sense, has seemed secondary to touch and sensation in Cixous's visceral texts. Cixous's is writing of the bloodstream, of the nerve-cells, of the interlacing of mind and body: she seeks to anatomize the imagination, to reach its interiority. The privileging of touch over vision is reminiscent of Luce Irigaray's position in *Ce Sexe qui n'en est pas un* (*This Sex Which Is Not One*) where she argues that feminine pleasure and signification come in touch rather than vision.[4] For Irigaray, women's place in the dominant masculine scopic regime has been (only) that of the beautiful object on display. This economy of surface and spectacle is countered in a new voicing of feminine pleasure, of female interiority and receptivity, all of which can also be traced in the language and image patterns of Cixous's texts.

The desire to approach the interior in textuality is linked specifically in Cixous, too, to textual innovation and to the desire to find in her texts an encounter with the unconscious, with dream, memory and the imagination. Interiority notably shifts away from the anatomically female, while guided by a set of values which may, nevertheless, guardedly be called 'feminine'.

I have been so taken with this reading of Cixous that I have long failed to see the visual return to be rewritten in her texts. For a female film critic, any fixed designation of scopophilia, or pleasure in looking, as exclusively masculine is troubling indeed. Feminist film theory has been concerned with re-thinking the way women look at films and asserting the possibility of a female gaze.[5] A lot is at stake, then, in thinking vision in the feminine. Cixous herself, despite her seeming veiling and avoidance of the visual, may be seen to aid this enterprise. Notably her approach to the visual is in keeping with the deconstructive move in her work as a whole. We begin with the binary of vision and touch which Irigaray sees in hierarchical and gendered terms. Cixous may appear to privilege the recessive term, making the sense of touch make sense and meaning in her texts. Yet touch is not explored to the exclusion of vision: the two gradually come to inhabit one another in her writing. This is the synaesthesia of Cixous's textuality, it is also a political gesture in the attempt to reclaim and rethink a feminine vision.

This re-vision of the scopic is witnessed in some of Cixous's most recent writing in her overt turn to the visual arts. Consider the essays collected in *Stigmata, Escaping Texts*,[6] in particular the first of these, 'Bathsheba or the interior Bible'. Here Cixous explores a new approach to painting and the visual arts through discussion of Rembrandt's *Bathsheba bathing*. This is a painting which both belongs to and differs from the tradition of male representation of the female nude which is in part source of Irigaray's very mistrust of a masculine scopic economy. *Bathsheba bathing* is reproduced in John Berger's *Ways of Seeing* and might be designated one of those paintings in which, in his terms, the woman painted is no longer a nude but a loved woman, more or less naked. Berger claims that: 'Among the hundreds of thousands of nudes which make up the tradition there are perhaps a hundred of these exceptions. In each case a painter's personal vision of the particular women he is painting is so strong that it makes no allowance for the spectator'.[7] His intimation of the difference in *Bathsheba bathing* seems important but intuitive rather than explanatory. Berger's claims for the painting, convincing though they seem, are still invested in an economy dependent on the male artist and female model/nude. Love is seen to rescue the relation and representation from the gaudy trappings of spectacle and exploitation.

Cixous will take us far closer to the painting, while still respecting and reflecting on the very exclusion of the spectator of which Berger speaks. In 'Bathsheba or the interior Bible', Cixous makes us think about how a woman can look at a painting, at how she can adopt and undo the viewing positions of the heterosexual male desiring spectator. Cixous writes: 'This female nude is not a nude. She is not made – not painted – to be seen nude. Precisely her – Bathsheba. She who was seen. Should not have been seen. She who is perceived. From afar'.[8] Each break in the sentence, in the flux of ideas, each new search for precision re-positions Bathsheba and the viewer's distance from her. Cixous's act of viewing depends on the recognition of the fissures of vision, on what is not seen, on the ways in which painting, and an approach to painting, can work to deny and undermine the culture of spectacle which fixes the female form as object of desire. For Cixous, in *Bathsheba bathing*: 'There is no smile: no exterior. No face that lets itself be looked at. That knows it is looked at. No face. No surface. No scene. Everything is in the interior. No representation' (5). Vision depends on the recognition of its failure, the intimation of all that is hidden. Cixous focuses on the division between viewer and object viewed, be this internal or external, be that object the self or another. Again in 'Bathsheba or the interior Bible' Cixous writes, in parenthesis:

(What does a naked woman think about – her rapport to her body, always the slight attention, like a veil, the glance or the gaze. Whenever I am naked, I don't look at myself, I cast a glance my way (– the glance of the other, of you/me at me) – But no, Bathsheba does not look at her body. She is not before herself. She is not here. She is gone, behind her eyelids.) (8)

Vision, even of the self-image, is always mediated across distance within the parameters of mental perception. Thinking vision, for Cixous, is about thinking the image as other, and thinking the relation to that other. Respecting that relation, indeed.

Inner Cinema

This concern with re-thinking vision, with the interiority of vision, and with its renewed mapping of self/other relations, is found in retrospect throughout Cixous's writing. Moving away from exclusive focus on touch and the tactile in her texts, I have been struck by how far Cixous seeks to give access to the image patterns of the mind, to memory, consciousness and dream in a way which draws the possibility of vision and visuality into question. Vision is never assumed in Cixous, yet looking again at her texts I have come to find in their recesses an exploration of an 'inner cinema' which I find wholly remarkable.

Verena Andermatt Conley has used a cinematic image to evoke the process of reading Cixous. She writes: 'Reading Cixous is not unlike watching home movies with their repetitions, their hidden affect, their unedited totalizing of rushes or dailies, their over and underexposure, their blurry moments as well as their moments of genuine psychic intensity'.[9] This analogy seems sharply apt in defining the process and texture of Cixous's texts, their temporality, intermittence and intimacy. Yet I think too that Cixous goes further to re-play the home movie to make it also *unheimlich*, uncanny and inaccessible. Hers is the home movie of our thought patterns. She makes us question what can be seen in the cinema of the mind's eye, dwelling on the properties of that image and its involvement in a spatial and temporal mapping of identity.

Using imagery of the 'inner cinema' I am taking my cue from Cixous. In the one (informal) conversation I have held with her she denied any interest in film as medium or cinema as entertainment. Pressed, she would admit to liking the cinema of Satyajit Ray. Yet the viewing scenario offered in cinematic spectatorship appears of use to Cixous in the image patterns of her text. Spectatorship as relation (as theorized in psychoanalytic and feminist film theory) depends on physical distance and motor incapacity, yet mental proximity and activity through identification (both psychological and visual).[10] Cixous appears to use spectatorship as image to evoke the relation between the self as lover and her object of desire. Spectatorship offers this paradox of proximity and distance which fits it to the spectacle of adoration from afar, as well as psychical symbiosis, which is found in love in Cixous. Witness the image in *La Bataille d'Arcachon* where 'Je' tells us of Promethea: 'Elle est difficile à résumer. Il m'arrive de la regarder comme si j'étais au cinéma'[11] (She is difficult to resume. I find myself watching her as if I were at the cinema). This image is found too and explored in more complex terms in *Le Livre de Promethea*.

The cinematic image recurs in a passage where Cixous examines the possibility of knowing the other in her absence:

Quand elle n'est pas là je 'pense à' elle, diversement: parfois par évocation, je la vois, je me passe de longs et lents films imaginaires grandioses et grossissants qui me permettent de l'observer de très très près. Alors c'est comme si je tenais ma lune au bout de mon télescope. Je vois chaque pore, chaque mont, chaque ravin, chaque inflexion de voix, et je note. Parfois par filature: je la suis (mentalement) dans ses déplacements, dans ses activités, je la regarde telle que je ne la vois jamais en réalité, je la devine telle qu'elle est en mon absence.[12]

(When she isn't there I 'think about' her in various ways: sometimes I conjure her up, I see her, I show myself long slow imaginary movies, magnifying things to a mammoth scale so I can observe her very, very close up. Then it is like having my moon on the tip of my telescope. I see every pore, every mountain, every ravine, every inflection of her voice, and I take note. Sometimes I tail her: I follow her (mentally) wherever she goes, whatever she does, I watch her in a way I never see her in reality, I imagine how she is in my absence.)

Here a direct link is made between mental process and 'inner cinema'. These imaginary home movies are the matter of the lover's mind as she evokes Promethea. Activity and passivity are fused here as the lover, 'Je', is both projectionist and spectator. These long, slow reels of film are, it seems, at once the product of her imagination and of her memory. If imaginary, these images are supposedly under the lover's control; if mnemonic they may yet reveal a detail or facet of Promethea missed thus far. The lover specifies that these are magnifying images: she exploits the potential of film to disrupt spatial and temporal relations. In these reels, reality is slowed and enlarged (as in love). The lover is magnified (as Promethea is magnificent throughout her book). Yet this act of enlargement serves not merely to magnify the loved one, but to survey her, to make a visual inventory of her every part.

Cixous refocuses her visual metaphor moving from cinema to astronomy, and charting Promethea as lunar terrain. This shift in image emphasizes still further the distance between lover and loved one, the celestial dimensions of the desire described, and the scientific means which will aid its codification. Promethea appears here entirely visible: all the impressions she leaves, down to the finest inflections of her voice, are rendered visible surface. The literal visuality of this viewing scenario is placed under threat. The image shifts again and 'Je' proceeds, ingeniously, 'par filature'. Evoking spinning and thread, Cixous recalls the images of Ariadne which bind the text. Yet 'par filature' alludes too to surveillance, to the imitation of Promethea the lover will achieve in shadowing her, in following her every move, in imagination and at one remove. Viewing Promethea becomes a means to knowing her, to surveying her even in the absence of the self. Viewing is an addictive activity; note the voraciousness with which we are told in *Messie*:

Nous sommes nés pour voir, pour vouloir voir et ne pas pouvoir voir pour devoir à tout prix franchir l'ultime voile mais où est-il, est-il là-bas, tenture tendue entre ces continents et l'Autre? ou bien est-il dans mes yeux? Le nez sur toi muette je crie: je veux te voir! voir voir voir voir! (104)

(We are born to see, to want to see and not be able to see to need to pull back the last veil at all costs but where is it, is it over there, hanging stretched between these continents and the Other? Or is it in my eyes? Pressed against you silent I cry: I want to see you! to see see see see!)

Viewing is haunted by its own failure. Objective vision, tantalizingly luminous, is sought in the allusion to the photographic medium of cinema. Yet that allusion itself proves illusory. 'Je' has sought to see Promethea how she never sees her in reality. She must accept that her mental images of her loved one, her inner cinema, will always be de-realized, that Promethea will always be missing in her imagination. The viewing scenario continues:

Mais aujourd'hui, je m'aperçois que je la manque, oui, malgré moi je ne cesse de passer près d'elle sans la voir, une dérive pénible se produit, je ne m'obéis pas, je me penche à la fenêtre de ma mémoire, je ne la vois pas en réalité, je la vois dans un rêve étranger dont je ne sais comment me réveiller. (*Le Livre de Promethea*, 62)

(But today I am aware that I am not getting her right, yes, in spite of myself I keep coming very close without seeing her, I drift badly, I disobey myself, I lean out of the window of my memory, I do not see her in reality, I see her in an unfamiliar dream from which I cannot awaken.) (*The Book of Promethea*, 49)

Viewing is fissured, the viewing scenario becomes the inevitable scene of missing the other, of approaching her yet failing to reach her. Cixous evokes a compulsive repetition and frustration of desire. Rather than gaining access to the loved one in the objectivity of vision, 'Je' remains subject to the subjectivity of inner vision, her inner cinema, which resembles only ever a 'rêve étranger' (unfamiliar dream), an unconscious projection before which she remains fixed as a viewer.

Visual Analogues

I have looked for visual analogues for the 'longs et lents films imaginaires grandioses et grossissants' of which Cixous writes. I have found these analogues in a cinema of mourning (rather than in a cinema of desire as the subject matter on *Le Livre de Promethea* might suggest). I want to allude briefly to two recent films. The first is Agnès Varda's *Jacquot de Nantes* (1993) her tribute to her husband, Jacques Demy after his death.

Jacquot de Nantes is a film which expertly traces the possibilities of cinema as mnemonic device, of photographic images as fetishes which at once avow and deny the loss of a mourned loved one. One of the most poignant devices Varda uses takes the form of a series of very slow tracking shots across the body of Jacques Demy, recording his living body as transcript, as visual caress and reminder, preserving him, as it were, with a mind to his death. Brief episodes of this pre-emptive mourning punctuate the film. In one such set of images we watch the camera move down through Demy's hair and over his face, making an inventory, it seems, of his living physical features.

My second image of mourning represented is found in Krzysztof Kieslowski's *Trois Couleurs: Bleu* (1993). The protagonist, Julie, played by Juliette Binoche, has survived a car crash in which her husband and small daughter have been killed. In an early scene, Julie watches their funeral. Her face and its responses are framed in the film in extreme close-up. The funeral service continues and Julie gives more open, involuntary expression to her grief. As if respecting the intimacy, the unknowability of this, the camera now closes in on only parts of her face, her mouth, the cuts she still bears from the accident, her wet eyes. As emotion overcomes her, *Bleu* leads the viewer to approach Julie's grief, yet only ever allows us a partial image of her face, stressing too our separation from her, the enormity of her grief which cannot be viewed in its entirety.

This is the idiom of Cixous's imaginary cinema. The infinitely close, painstaking observation she evokes and requires is mnemonic and melancholy. Eroticism in Cixous, the relation to the loved one she celebrates, is reverent and fearful. Loss governs love relations, as the other is missed in order to be desired, as the other as missing is internalized and made a player in the inner cinema of the subject's mental processes and her self construction.

Cinema itself is a melancholy medium dependent on loss and denial: what defines the specifically cinematic scopic regime is the absence of the object seen.[13] The image on the screen functions as memory trace of the moment of filming. It is both made present by projection, yet defined as virtual and retrospective by virtue of the temporal *décalage* between filming and viewing. The space of the cinema screen seems both very close and definitively inaccessible. This is its relevance in the image patterns of Cixous's text.

Cixous and Memory

The passages cited from *Le Livre de Promethea* work to correlate, and potentially to confuse, vision, memory and dream, as if Cixous proposes the equivalence or indiscernibility of these moments of viewing and their respective virtual images. She emphasizes contamination as she emphasizes failure. The very lack of fixity, of codification of the mental processes is Cixous's subject in *Le Livre de Promethea*, as it is frequently elsewhere in her texts. *Le Livre de Promethea*, like Cixous's other texts, attempts in part to be a mnemonic text. It is a text which returns the death of the father to consciousness, which returns to this source of the identity of the self and her writing. Yet memory is not contained: it is immediately emotional and associative. 'Je' writes: 'J'ai trois peurs. J'ai une peur à mon père le juif, j'ai une peur de trois mille ans à sa mémoire et à la mémoire de son peuple' (40) (I have three fears. I have a fear from my father, the Jew; I have a three-thousand-year-old fear from his memory and the memory of his people) (30). By filiation, fear and its memory are interwoven with the history of a race and its grief. Cixous acknowledges the exorbitant patterns of her grief texts and her commemorative writing. 'Je' admits: 'J'ai une mémoire adoptive. Dans ma mémoire s'étend un camp de mémoires' (42) (My memory adopts. A memory camp spreads out in my memory) (32). Her memory is receptive, it is a historic memory and a traumatized memory. Loss is not limited for Cixous within the personal realm, but part of a public narrative. Yet she stresses the inaccessibility of that narrative, the failure of memory and imagination in the face of loss. Even access to an individual's trauma is faulty, as grief disrupts the recording mechanisms of the mind. This failure, these faultlines, will be drawn into focus in Cixous's texts in extreme close up. The cinema of the mind's eye, an individual's memory and imagination, becomes an apparatus for exploring ungrievable loss (both personal and public). For Cixous even this attempt to represent the subjective is open to failure, but is an ethical necessity.

Memory is insistent, yet deceptive in Cixous. 'Je' tells us: 'Je voudrais me laver la mémoire dans l'oubli' (42) (I would like to wash my memory in forgetting) (32). She seeks oblivion, unable to bear the pain of memory, yet manages only to find herself submerged in false memories. The self fails as projectionist. She remains instead as spectator fixed before false images which threaten always to overwhelm her, to be the site of false witnessing and the missing of the other. Loss and fear govern memory. The object of desire is missed in Cixous because she must be missing in order to be desired. Her loss must be made present, yet ungrievable. In this sense melancholia determines amorous relations in Cixous. What troubles me here is the relation between the mnemonic text (or text of memory and mourning) and the erotic text in *Le Livre de Promethea* that this supposes. We may wonder what is at stake in thinking their inter-relation.

Gender and Melancholia

Throughout her work, and most recently in 'Melancholy Gender/Refused Identification', Judith Butler has made use of Freud's observations on mourning and melancholia in order 'to think of gender as a kind of melancholy, or as one of melancholy's effects'.[14] She reminds us that 'Freud himself acknowledged that melancholy, the unfinished process of grieving, is central to the formation of the identifications that form the ego' (132). Butler asserts further that 'what Freud (...) calls the "character of the ego" appears to be the sedimentation of objects loved and lost, the archaeological remainder, as it were, of unresolved grief' (133). This sedimentation may be a remainder of unresolved grief, but identifications also act as reminders of unresolved grief. This Butler stresses, arguing that 'the lost object continues to haunt and inhabit the ego' (134). Melancholic incorporation is always already double. Identification becomes a means of preserving a lost object in a desperate attempt to maintain its presence, yet loss is inevitably acknowledged in the very inception of the move to refuse distance from the loved object. For Butler, 'If in melancholia a loss is refused, it is not for that reason abolished. Internalization preserves loss in the psyche' (134). Put another way, internalization may disavow loss, yet that disavowal will arguably always be haunted by the death or absence it denies.

Writing about mourning and melancholia, Butler talks very little about literal grief. One exception is an aside where she elaborates on 'the predicament of living in a culture which can mourn the loss of homosexual attachment only with great difficulty' (138). She observes: 'This problematic is made all the more acute when we consider the ravages of AIDS, and the task of finding a public occasion and language in which to grieve this seemingly endless number of deaths' (138). The aside seems important politically with relation to Butler's critique of heterosexist society. Yet I find it compelling too, and all too brief, in its glancing allusion to death and the literal process of mourning. The example serves to give us pause in Butler's argument and render it suddenly acute and in the moment. It reminds us of loss as visceral and irrevocable.

This is a reminder which I think is necessary, where loss and mourning are deployed as mechanism or metaphor by which the constitution of the self is explained. This is a reminder we are offered by Cixous for whom the process of mourning is made present. She works to create an unrelenting text, a text which reminds its readers insistently and incessantly of the painful processes of self construction, whereby loss is both internalized and refused, where the self emerges as a product of both memory and desire. What Cixous refuses, precisely, is to allow the pain and disorientation of loss to be disregarded. Cixous's fictions are consistent with Freudian and queer theoretical projections of the constitution of identity. Yet her work moves further to literalize their terms. Cixous refuses to let us forget the ways in which identification is melancholy, is response to ungrievable loss. Identity is palpably mournful for Cixous; its denials are avowed.

This literalization takes its source in the literal loss of the father. She explores the melancholy of becoming a self in a drama where loss takes the form not merely of separation or refusal but of literal death. The death of the father as it returns in Cixous's texts allows them painfully to exceed the normative model of gender melancholy Butler constructs and critiques. The melancholy constitution of the self Cixous echoes, refuses any fixed division between desire and identification. The father remains object of desire as his spectre is internalized. Desire is maintained in the refusal of his loss, yet that melancholy denial is itself a process of incorporation and identification by which the self is constituted. The self in Cixous is the product of conflicted and differential relations. It is also, very graphically, a product of literal mourning and distress. And it is here that Cixous outstrips Butler in imagining the implications of a theory of melancholy gender. Desiring relations in Cixous are determined by the love relation which has early been foreclosed by loss and which remains ungrievable. Desire itself becomes a part of a process of mourning.

Conclusion

The scopic is not denied by Cixous in her evocation of love between women, as I have thought previously. Rather the scopic is re-viewed as regime of loss, melancholy and distance. Cixous may productively and politically refuse the objectification of the body, the voyeurism and exhibitionism which have seemed to inhere in cinema (and other visual art forms). Yet she does not refuse vision itself. Rather she shows the ways in which our view of cinema may be inflected by a renewed awareness of the proximity between the visual traces of film and the visual traces of our imagination, our mind's eye, our memory. Cixous evokes imaginary films as elsewhere she evokes imaginary memories, claiming the permeability and uncertainty of all mental process.

Both cinema and memory arguably work to re-present and represent what is now missing. This defines their melancholia. Memory in Cixous appears exorbitant, contaminating and uncontainable. Its dictates determine desiring relations where the experience of loss in desire is repeated and loss itself becomes a determinant of desire. Here her texts hint at the horror of an analogy between identity formation and melancholia. Cixous refuses to claim the universality of this melancholia, but renders it instead entirely personal and the product of a literal drama of loss. This is the inner cinema to which she gives us access, refusing to spare us its pain and failures. Cixous creates missing images in her texts in an ethical, even unbearable, avowal of ungrievable loss.

EMMA WILSON
Corpus Christi College, Cambridge

NOTES

1 Hélène Cixous, *Messie* (Paris, Editions des femmes, 1996), p. 29. Translations are my own unless otherwise stated.
2 Emma Wilson, 'Hélène Cixous: An Erotics of the Feminine', in *French Erotic Fiction: Women's Desiring Writing, 1880-1990*, edited by Alex Hughes and Kate Ince (Oxford, Berg, 1996), pp. 121-45.
3 Emma Wilson, *Sexuality and the Reading Encounter* (Oxford, Clarendon Press, 1996).
4 Luce Irigaray, *Ce Sexe qui n'en est pas un* (Paris, Editions de Minuit, 1977); *This Sex Which Is Not One*, translated by Catherine Porter with Carolyn Burke (Ithaca, Cornell University Press, 1985).
5 See Linda Williams, *Viewing Positions: Ways of Seeing Film* (New Brunswick, N.J., Rutgers University Press, 1995) and Judith Mayne, *Cinema and Spectatorship* (London and New York, Routledge, 1993).
6 Hélène Cixous, *Stigmata: Escaping Texts* (London and New York, Routledge, 1998).
7 John Berger, *Ways of Seeing* (London, British Broadcasting Corporation/ Penguin, 1972), p. 57.
8 Hélène Cixous, 'Bathsheba or the interior Bible', translated by Catherine A.F. MacGillivray, in *Stigmata: Escaping Texts*, pp. 3-19 (p. 3).
9 Verena Andermatt Conley, *Hélène Cixous* (Hemel Hempstead, Harvester Wheatsheaf [Modern Cultural Theorists], 1992), p. 70.
10 Here I refer to the model of viewing relations constructed by Christian Metz in *Psychoanalysis and Cinema*: The Imaginary Signifier, translated by Celia Britton, Annwyl Williams, Ben Brewster and Alfred Guzzetti (London, Macmillan, 1982).
11 Hélène Cixous, *La Bataille d'Arcachon* (Laval, Québec, Editions Trois, 1986), p. 48.
12 Hélène Cixous, *Le Livre de Promethea* (Paris, Gallimard, 1983), p. 62; *The Book of Promethea*, translated and with an introduction by Betsy Wing (Lincoln and London, University of Nebraska Press, 1991), p. 49.
13 See André Bazin, *Qu'est-ce que le cinéma?* (Paris, Editions du Cerf, 1975) and Christian Metz, *Psychoanalysis and Cinema*.
14 Judith Butler, *The Psychic Life of Power: Theories of Subjection* (Stanford, California, Stanford University Press, 1997), p. 132.

At the Time of Writing Theatre: Cixous's Absolute Present

Quelle heure est-il? C'est la question clé du théâtre.[1]
(What time is it? This is the key question of the theatre.)

The time and space of classical theatre are rejected in both Cixous's early writings on theatre and in productions of her first plays.[2] In the early eighties, the theatre re-enters Cixous's work not through the experience of its practice, nor as the subject of textual study, but within the context of her exploration and reformulation of the relationship between writer and text; the process of writing. Her approach to the theatre from this point on does not sustain a critical engagement with the temporal and spatial structures of conventional theatre itself (although her collaborations with the Théâtre du Soleil could be read in this light) but implicates this same theatrical form in her search for a mode of writing which is capable of responding to two central concerns of her aesthetics; the representation of difference and the relationship between writing and time.

The essays included in the volume Théâtre,[3] those published alongside *L'Indiade ou l'Inde de leurs rêves*[4] and a piece 'De la scène de l'Inconscient à la scène de l'Histoire',[5] constitute the main examples of a discourse which has dominated Cixous's discussion of, and approach to, the theatre since the mid 1980s. Indeed Cixous's writing *on* the theatre and her own writing for the theatre work within a largely classical frame of textual reference to Shakespearean and Greek tragedy. In her writing on the theatre there is no reference to modes of avant garde or radical political theatre which might, at the very least, question the positing of a homogenous audience response and the necessarily beneficial outcome of conventional suspension of belief and experience of catharsis. Cixous's writing on the theatre develops a notion of generic specificity which was hitherto absent from her aesthetics as she maintains throughout a clear distinction between the process of writing for the theatre and writing in other genres. In these texts the theatre as form becomes inseparable from the process of writing for the theatre and both are seen to permit different relationships to time and space which respond to Cixous's ideal mode of writing. Firstly the desire to articulate new approaches to alterity, the re-mapping of different relationships between self and other, author and text, author and reader and secondly the desire to reconcile temporal conflicts in her work by accommodating both writing as inscription of the past, fulfilling poetic and ethical drives to preserve memory, and writing as ongoing process, ever-open and incomplete. It is the second of these concerns that I wish to focus on here.

Within Cixous's aesthetics theatre has become established as a utopian site of intersubjective relations, a model determined by the process of writing and reproduced, through parallel moves, between author and text, author and audience, audience and characters. Cixous acclaims the theatre as a space in which author, actor and audience become capable of suspending their exclusive identities and occupying the place of the other:

Ecrire pour le théâtre: il faut éloigner de soi, partir, voyager longtemps dans l'obscurité, jusqu'à ne plus savoir où l'on est, qui l'on est, c'est très difficile... jusqu'à se réveiller, métamorphosé en quelqu'un que je n'ai jamais rencontré... ('Le Chemin de légende', 7)

(To write for the theatre you must leave yourself behind, you must set out, travel for a long time in darkness, until you no longer know where you are, nor who you are, it's very difficult... until you awake, having metamorphosed into someone that you have never met...)

Cixous expresses such transformations in predominantly spatial terms, the self withdraws and the author has 'l'honneur d'être la scène de l'autre'[6] (the honour of becoming the scene of the other). Generic specificity and generic erasure maintain an uneasy coexistence in many of Cixous's statements on theatre as, whilst the importance of the experience of dramatic production as source for a model of writing is asserted, the central performance, in terms of form and thematic content, seems to remain that of the theatricalized writing of the text – the scene of writing rather than the scene of the theatre. Cixous asserts the liberating potential of theatre as offering the possibility of radical displacement and fluid subject identification: 'Le théâtre est le palais d'autrui. Il vit du désir de l'autre, de tous les autres. Et du désir du désir des autres: du public, des comédiens' ('L'Incarnation', 260) (The theatre is the palace of others. It lives on the desire of the other, of all others. And of the desire for the desire of others: of the public, of the actors). Yet as I argue elsewhere,[7] the projected territories of Cixous's theatre can be read as the spaces of writing in which the central protagonist represents an increasingly explicit poet figure and the dramatic denouement serves to assert the ethical importance of their role in communicating with humanity. The presentation of the theatrical performance as emancipatory space for audience and actor and the consequent different relationship to the other engendered in writing for the theatre is accompanied by a persistent reference to the importance of the temporal specificities of writing for the theatre and of the theatrical experience. I want to explore the tensions between the temporally-motivated imperatives of writing, the recording of 'Histoire' (both History and personal narrative in Cixous's theatre) and the specific temporal nature of theatre in Cixous's aesthetics.

The communal time created in/by the performance is important to Cixous's adoption of the theatre as a form through which, she claims, humanity can rediscover itself. Her discourse is clearly reminiscent of more radical Artaudian claims for the potential of communal catharsis. As she asserts:

Le Théâtre est (au) Présent. Doit toujours être au présent. C'est sa chance. A chaque moment le présent éclate. Le présent est d'un noir brillant. On avance le coeur battant de ne pas savoir ce qui va arriver. Et cet imprévisible qui nous tient en haleine, nous soulève, nous transporte au-dessus de nous-mêmes, c'est la vie même. Au théâtre le public n'en sait pas plus que le personnage sur lui-même. Personne ne précède. Ensemble on ne comprend pas. Ensemble on hésite. Cela crée entre tous l'obscure et frémissante complicité archaïque. ('Le Chemin de légende', 10)

(The Theatre is (in the) Present. It must always be in the present. That's its privilege. At each moment the present explodes. The present is a brilliant blackness. We move forward, our hearts beating from not knowing what is going to happen. And this unpredictability that keeps us alive, lifts us up, transports us beyond ourselves, is life itself. In the theatre the audience know no more than the character about himself. No-one is ahead. Together we don't understand. Together we hesitate. This creates the dark and thrilling ancient complicity amongst us all.)

This shared time of performance, and the fact that each performance is inevitably and infinitely different, encourages Cixous to present theatre as a healing social ritual capable of combating the pernicious alienation and inherently repetitious nature of contemporary mass-media: 'le théâtre est l'espace où l'être humain s'éprouve comme un atome du cosmos, comme une minute du Temps, comme une question dans le multimillénaire dialogue des hommes avec les dieux...'[8] (The theatre is the space where human beings experience themselves as atoms of the cosmos, as minutes in Time, as questions in the infinite dialogue of Man with the gods...). Cixous distinguishes clearly between writing 'fictions' and writing for the theatre and the act of writing for the theatre is thus closely associated in temporal terms with the theatrical performance itself:

Quand j'écris un texte littéraire à ma façon, c'est une tapisserie, je tisse tranquillement à l'horizontale et ce sont les mots, les phrases qui me conduisent. Là c'est le contraire. Le théâtre c'est debout, verticalement, tout de suite. Entrent les personnages...J'ai trente secondes pour que le public ait compris les enjeux de cette scène...Il faut donc essayer d'écrire comme une flèche, et droit au coeur du personnage. Vraiment tout le contraire de mes livres qui sont faits de lenteur. Tout doit être aigu, tendu, j'ai dû me mettre à l'école du théâtre.[9]

(When I write a literary text in my own way, it's a tapestry, I weave calmly, horizontally and it is the words, the phrases that guide me. Here, it's the opposite. The theatre is up on its feet, vertically, immediately. In come the characters...I have thirty seconds to make the public understand what is at stake in this scene...You must therefore try to write like an arrow, straight to the heart of the characters. Really the complete opposite to my books which are made with/of slowness. Everything must be sharp, tense, I have had to enrol myself in the school of theatre.)

Writing for the theatre is described by Cixous as a more immediate, shared experience than writing in other forms, the theatrical experience is thus projected into the writing of the play. Theatre's conventional suspension of the audience in intradiegetic time and space, and the immediate response of the audience to the performance, and so to the text, is seen by Cixous to influence the writing process, providing a model for an ideal 'writing in the present': 'Arriver à être au présent absolu, c'est le charme du théâtre et sa nécessité. Ecrire le présent dans le texte poétique, c'est acrobatique'[10] (The ability to exist in the absolute present is the charm and the necessity of the theatre. Writing the absolute present in the poetic text is an acrobatic feat). The recurrent references to writing theatre as 'writing in the present' constitute a counterpart to the insistence throughout Cixous's oeuvre on the power and role of writing as a 'combat with bereavement'[11] in inscribing the past and ensuring the support of personal and cultural memory. Indeed, in her writing on the theatre, questions of mortality and inscription persist:

Et la substance magique du théâtre: le Temps. Du vrai temps, avec toutes les secondes (non, il n'y a pas de temps dans la fiction, donc pas de suspens terrifié), la sensation de 'ça va arriver!', du 'il est encore temps!', du 'ça pourrait encore ne pas arriver'; et toujours le pas léger de la mort qui approche, l'imminence, – et puis: le coup![12]

(And the magic ingredient of theatre: Time. Real time, with all its seconds (no, there is no time in fiction, and so no terrified suspense) the feeling that 'it's going to happen', that 'there's still time!', that 'it still might not happen'; and always the light step of approaching death, imminence – and then the final blow!)

The theatre is identified by Cixous as the form and site in which the inevitability of temporal movement is most keenly experienced, yet this movement is countered in her avowed motivation in writing plays as her recent comments reveal: 'Why do I write theatre? Because I am haunted, by those who return, who rise up... for the joy of being the scene of their return'.[13] For Cixous, the theatre is also implicated in this project as a 'manifestation au présent de la mémoire' (Cerisy) (the appearance of memory in the present) and in the ethical imperatives behind this. The theatre is therefore expected to assert an absolute present, as experienced both by the audience in the time-span of the play (eight hours over two consecutive evenings in the case of *La Ville parjure*) and the writer performing the theatrical text, whilst the narratives of Cixous's plays foreground the importance of inscription of the past in the present. This dual concern constitutes, I would argue, one of the central themes of Cixous's dramatic oeuvre and generates a tension in her plays as her theatre searches for temporal solutions which would allow both past and present to coexist equally. The desire to share an untold story,[14] to convey to the audience the importance of maintaining the past in the present through both writing and performance, must find a harmonious simultaneity with the need to emphasize both the potential of the absolute present of the performance and the audience's communal time of catharsis. Such temporal acrobatics have invested many of Cixous's plays with a sense of timelessness, or of being beyond time, time zones which may indeed hinder engagement with ethical and political intentions of the plays.

The proliferation in Cixous's recent theatre of characters returning from the dead, of scenes set in apparent representations of an afterlife, or at least a realm situated beyond temporal and mortal limitations, is striking. Cixous's early plays, however, do not articulate this concern. Although they posit the existence of an elsewhere, perhaps a feminine Imaginary, their primary engagement remains a challenge to the conventional temporal frame of the theatrical form itself, militant disruptions of spatial unity and chronological linearity. This is achieved either through the representation of simultaneous zones of spatial and temporal perception employed in *Portrait de Dora*[15] or the adoption of the Classical unities to foreground theatre's repression of the subject-in-process.[16]

Cixous's return to the theatrical form in the mid-eighties seems to have been partly motivated by the desire to engage with History and to represent contemporary historical events in an epic mode, drawing on Shakespearean history plays as a model: 'Etre un Théâtre de l'Histoire, c'est sans doute l'ambition la plus noble du théâtre, sinon peut-être sa vocation' (*Théâtre/Public*, 24) (To be a theatre of History, is undoubtedly theatre's noblest aim, if not its vocation). These projects, epic dramas on the partition of India[17] and recent Cambodian history,[18] were commissioned by the Théâtre du Soleil, and were clearly hugely influenced by the work undertaken by Ariane Mnouchkine and the Théâtre du Soleil during this period.[19] There is not room here to discuss the aesthetic and political consequences of these plays' employment of specific geographical and historical events to frame allegories of writing, a move which runs the risk of presenting other spaces and subjectivities through an ultimately essentializing dialectic that at times recalls the tropes of colonial discourse.[20] Nonetheless, this danger is replicated in the representation of time within the plays. Cambodia and India are represented as eternal sites through which a dual reading of 'histoire', the representation of both national History and personal narrative might be possible. The desire to ensure that these stories are told, to 'wrest one's prey from forgetfulness' ('Writing blind', 13), is encapsulated by the numerous characters who return from the dead to participate in events, an emphatic refusal to be forgotten. If Cixous's project of writing originates in an intensely personal urge to 'weave time' in response to her father's death ('Writing blind', 16), then it is the character of Suramarit, Sihanouk's deceased father, who first performs this reincarnation in her theatre.[21] The increasing numbers of ghostly presences on the stage serves to underline the scale of loss suffered by the Cambodian people whilst also offering hope in their ability to resist the forced erasure of cultural memory, a resistance mirrored by Cixous's play itself. Yet the temporal mode of these two plays is complex. The spatial evocation of both Cambodia and India in the Théâtre du Soleil's productions clearly strove to assert their cultural differences but, as Morag Shiach points out, treads a fine line between 'recognition and strangeness: a dual response characteristic not just of the uncanny, but also of the cultural legacies of colonialism'.[22] The temporal scene replicates this model as the peoples of India and Cambodia are represented as having different relationships to time and indeed to mortality, the trope of resistance becomes somewhat undermined by the sense of an eternal otherness which transcends History.

Cixous's theatre has continued to dramatize narratives of those repressed or erased from cultural memory, those in danger of being forgotten. 'Voile noire, voile blanche/Black Sail, White Sail'[23] is clearly set in the Soviet Union during Stalin's rule, and the importance of the daily struggle to preserve cultural memory is signified by the dramatis personae which includes two categories; the 'Absent-presences' and the 'Present-absences', statuses which both transcend mortality and define the characters' position in this struggle. The present in the play is dominated by the need of the two central protagonists, the writers Anna Akhmatova and Nadezhda Mandelshtam, to ensure the survival of poetry and memory, and the desire to foresee the future. The play's central theme is resistance, both to death and censorship, and is evident in the persistent undermining of boundaries between the dead and the living; those dead but living on through their poetry, the living death described by those erased from cultural memory by brutal censorship and the disappeared who are neither living nor dead. Akhmatova journeys to and from Moscow, the frozen River Neva thaws (both of course potent tropes in Russian culture) yet the characters remain curiously suspended in time, both guardians and servants of the past attendant on uncertain future change. In the final scene the writers address the audience across time in a plea for news of their status 'from the shores of the twenty-first century' ('Voile noire, voile blanche', 350) inhabiting a temporal limbo between a lack of cultural inscription to ensure the survival of the past and a present to which they apparently have no access. They remain curiously outside of time, a device of dramatic closure yet temporal abstraction which has become recurrent in Cixous's theatre.

La Ville parjure ou le reveil des Erinyes,[24] a play which imbues a contemporary medical and political scandal with the status of classical tragedy, through the intervention of the Furies in the recent scandal over the supply of contaminated blood to haemophiliacs in France, is also preoccupied with questions of mortality, transcendence and the power of writing to bear witness, to foster cultural memory. The central setting of the play, the cemetery in which the bereaved mother seeks asylum, provides a marginal site in terms of its inhabitants' status within the dominant political regime, yet the production also encourages the audience's hesitance over whether these characters are simply sheltering in the cemetery or are, in fact, more permanent residents. The guardian,

Aeschylus (here, a woman) has inscribed the names of murdered writers on the cemetery walls. The two children, killed by medical negligence, return from the dead to visit their mother in two pivotal scenes whose emotive power is heightened by their very silence. The theatre is clearly implicated here in the power of its own temporal specificity, Cixous's goal of the 'absolute present', and ensures the telling of this story, yet the final message of the play, an appeal to the audience to register the scale of such tragedies and to protest is set outside of time.

The State authorities sanction the flooding of the cemetery, a symbolic cleansing in which the main, mortal protagonists are killed. The final scene is set in the 'heavens' a luxurious 'kingdom of Night' from where Aeschylus, the Mother and the two children, seemingly relieved of the burden of living, survey the world that they have left. In Mnouchkine's production, the main lights went down and the ceiling of the Cartoucherie was suddenly illuminated by hundreds of tiny lights, representing the stars and effecting a magical transformation that abruptly changed the tone of the play. This temporal and spatial beyond clearly enables the Mother to impart her final message to the audience with maximum ethical authority as it comes from beyond the grave yet this final scene contrasts so sharply with the visual and verbal codes of the rest of the play that it remains, I would argue, extremely difficult for the audience to assimilate. The sudden further temporal abstraction can be seen to have a parallel effect to the potentially demobilizing and conservative capacity of myth and mythmaking, here the danger of narrative disempowerment conferred through the mythologization of contemporary events.[25] The play's awakening of the Furies in protest against the apparent acceptance of contemporary tragedies remains potent, and the articulation of the desperate choice between justice and revenge is emphatically relevant, yet I would argue that these far-reaching aspects are diluted by the temporal chasm which opens up between audience and protagonists at the end of the play.

The evocation of intertexts of Classical tragedy as a defence against the anaesthetic effects of mass-media coverage of contemporary injustices remains central to Cixous's work. The presence of immortal figures from Classical Greek mythology in *La Ville parjure* which serves further to highlight questions of mortality is maintained through the inclusion of Nordic gods in *L'Histoire (qu'on ne connaîtra jamais)*.[26] Through its persistent focus on relationships between time and writing, process and text, this play, which was first performed in 1994 (directed by Daniel Mesguich at the Théâtre de l'Odéon) presents a fascinating site for an exploration of the temporal zones of Cixous's theatre. The play's temporal messages are complex, indeed the title itself constitutes a temporal puzzle – a narrative that denies its own presence, remaining elusive and forever incomplete.

The play, which works with the intertext of Wagner's *Niebelungen*, is peopled by gods and immortal beings, several of whom are capable of manipulating time for their own ends. The secret narrative at the heart of Cixous's play is that of Sigfrid and Brunhild's passion, a narrative that has been erased from Sigfrid's memory by a magic potion but which continues to haunt Brunhild, and threatens to undermine the state visit of Sigfrid and Kriemhild to the court of Brunhild and Gunther. The lack of mutual inscription of this memory, a conflict between inscription and erasure, past and present, profoundly disturbs Brunhild's identity. She expresses this as the pain of a temporal exile:

Ni présent, ni passé, où vivre?
Il faut oublier, trancher la vie au collet, faire comme s'il n'y avait jamais eu la vie, trancher le morceau vivant et recoudre le corps, comme si jamais
Alors renoué avec le passé d'avant le passé. (145)

(No present, no past, where am I to live? I must forget, cut the throat of life, act as if life had never existed, cut out the living part and stitch up the body, as if (n)ever. So reconnect with the past that came before the past)

Incapable of such mutilation of the self and so unable to survive in this present without a past, Brunhild's greatest desire is to be forgotten herself. In Mesguich's production, which employed a consistent visual notation of cloth and fabric to signify narrative, Brunhild withdraws from the front of the stage as her gown is recuperated into a luxurious red curtain, the repressed yet utopian past from which her present existence cannot be separated.

The destructive consequences of the non-inscription of Brunhild's story is paralleled with the frustrated desire of the poet Snorri Sturlusson to construct a closed narrative from the continuous present of unfolding events. Sturlusson's obsession with the production of finished works to combat his own mortality is emphasized from the very beginning of the play (15) and represented onstage by towers of books reaching precariously towards the heavens, a bid to live on through his work. This mode of writing is presented as misguided, Sturlusson fails to portray events as he refuses to allow himself to be carried along with the present, thinking he can merely observe and relate a finished narrative. A change in Sturlusson's relationship to time (his death) enables him, however, to participate in the absolute present of the theatre. As Cixous states explicitly in the programme notes: 'Le passé qui était son objet de désir, le cède au présent' (The past which was his object of desire yields it to the present). This acceptance of the present brings with it an acceptance of mortality that Cixous associates with writing: 'Writing is learning to die. It's learning not to be afraid, in other words to live at the extremity of life, which is what the dead, death, give us'.[27] Sturlusson is murdered yet returns to change the course of events and break the narrative's cycle of murderous revenge. The present of the theatre and the process of writing are here presented as inseparable in their openness to change and in the successfulness of their intervention in the closed narrative of the *Niebelungen*. Sturlusson's lament in the final scene, 'Personne ne racontera jamais notre histoire' (184) (No-one will ever tell our story), forms an ironic reference to Cixous's play and, it could be argued, jolts the audience out of the present of the theatre to remind them of the creation of the written text of the play in the past.[28] However, the relationship of the poet to time within the play remains clear, Sturlusson must accept mortality and allow it to inhabit and inform his approach to writing. The haunting yet remote afterlives of the preceding plays are now replaced by the present of the writing process which, aligned with the present of the theatre, celebrates openness to change whilst bearing witness to Cixous's continuing belief in the ability of writing to maintain witness to the past in the present.

Cixous's oeuvre remains preoccupied with the telling of time and the power of the poetic to 'weave time' to ensure that the traces of memory (both personal and cultural) live in the present of writing.[29] Her theatre reveals a central tension as author and audience are constantly repositioned between shifting temporal planes, between the ethical role of writing to inscribe memory, to insure the reception of things past, and the attempt to maintain the liberating power of the absolute present of the theatre in both writing and performance. This tension manifests itself in the proliferation of final scenes in Cixous's theatre which take place in temporal beyonds removed from both the temporal setting of the past and the present of inscription. This search for a site in which the past and present can comfortably coexist culminates in the dramatization of the time of writing in *L'Histoire (qu'on ne connaîtra jamais)*. Capable of accommodating both the need for inscription of the past and the present's desire to evade closure, Cixous's engagement with the theatre has engendered and inspired a temporal acrobatics in her search for a mode of writing, perhaps a 'theatre of writing', from which it has become inseparable. This fascinating interplay continues at the time of writing.

JULIA DOBSON
University of Wolverhampton

NOTES

1. Hélène Cixous, unpublished seminar archive (4 March 1989).
2. See Hélène Cixous, 'Aller à la mer', *Le Monde* (28 April 1977).
3. Hélène Cixous, 'Le Chemin de légende', in *Théâtre*, (Paris, des femmes, 1986), pp. 7-11.
4. Hélène Cixous, 'Ecrits sur le théâtre', in *L'Indiade ou l'Inde de leurs rêves* (Paris, Théâtre du Soleil, 1987), pp. 247-78.
5. Hélène Cixous, 'De la scène de l'Inconscient à la scène de l'Histoire', in *Hélène Cixous, chemins d'une écriture*, edited by Françoise van Rossum-Guyon and Myriam Díaz-Diocaretz, (Vincennes, Presses Universitaires de Vincennes, 1990), pp. 15-34.
6. Hélène Cixous, 'L'Incarnation', in *L'Indiade ou l'Inde de leurs rêves*, p. 260.
7. See Julia Dobson, 'The Scene of Writing: The Representation of Poetic Identity in Cixous's Recent Theatre', *Theatre Research International* 23:3 (1998), 255-60.
8. Hélène Cixous, 'L'Ourse, la Tombe, les Etoiles', in *L'Indiade ou l'Inde de leurs rêves*, p. 248.
9. Hélène Cixous, Interview, *Théâtre / Public* 68 (1986), 19-24 (24).
10. Françoise van Rossum-Guyon, 'A propos de *Manne*: Entretien avec Hélène Cixous', in *Hélène Cixous, chemins d'une écriture*, pp. 213-34 (p. 227).
11. Hélène Cixous, 'Writing Blind', *Triquarterly* 97 (1996), 7-20 (13).
12. Hélène Cixous, 'A Quoi Bon le Théâtre?', *Théâtre Ouvert: Vingt Ans* (July 1991), 17-18.
13. Hélène Cixous, Roundtable on theatre, Cerisy la Salle, July 1998 .
14. This is reflected in two play titles *L'Histoire terrible mais inachevée de Norodom Sihanouk, roi du Cambodge* (*The Terrible but Unfinished Story of Norodom Sihanouk, King of Cambodia*) and *L'Histoire (qu'on ne connaîtra jamais)* (*The Story (that we will never know)*).
15. Hélène Cixous, *Portrait de Dora* (Paris, des femmes, 1976).
16. Hélène Cixous, *Le Nom d'Oedipe. Chant du corps interdit* (Paris, des femmes, 1978).
17. Hélène Cixous, *L'Indiade ou L'Inde de leurs rêves* (Paris, Théâtre du Soleil, 1987).
18. Hélène Cixous, *L'Histoire terrible mais inachevée de Norodom Sihanouk, roi du Cambodge* (Paris, Théâtre du Soleil, 1985).
19. For further details see David Bradby and Annie Sparks, *Mise en Scène: French Theatre Now*, (London, Methuen, 1997), pp. 92-7.

20 For further discussion of these aspects see: Anne-Marie Picard, 'L'Indiade ou l'Inde de leurs rêves', *Dalhousie French Studies* 17 (1989), 17-26; Jennifer Birkett, 'The Limits of Language: the Theatre of Hélène Cixous', in *Voices in the Air: French Dramatists and the Resources of Language*, edited by John Dunkley and Bill Kirton (Glasgow, University of Glasgow French and German Publications, 1992).
21 See Hélène Cixous, 'De la scène de l'Inconscient à la scène de l'Histoire', p. 30.
22 Morag Shiach, *Hélène Cixous: A Politics of Writing* (London and New York, Routledge, 1991), p. 135.
23 Hélène Cixous, 'Voile noire, voile blanche/Black Sail, White Sail', translated by Catherine A. F. MacGillivray, *New Literary History* 25 (2) (1994), 219-354.
24 Hélène Cixous, *La Ville parjure ou le reveil des Erinyes* (Paris, Théâtre du Soleil, 1994).
25 For a more detailed discussion of Cixous's employment of myth, see Julia Dobson, 'The Theatre of the Self: Poetic Identity in the Plays of Hélène Cixous and Marina Tsvetaeva' (unpublished PhD thesis, University of Nottingham, 1996).
26 Hélène Cixous, *L'Histoire (qu'on ne connaîtra jamais)* (Paris, des femmes, 1994).
27 Hélène Cixous, 'The School of the Dead', in *Three Steps on the Ladder of Writing* (New York, Columbia University Press, 1993), pp. 1-55 (p. 10).
28 This argument is central to discussions of Cixous's projection of her own poetic identity in her theatre. See Julia Dobson, 'The Scene of Writing: The Representation of Poetic Identity in Cixous's Recent Theatre'.
29 Temporal play is central to *Or, les lettres de mon père* (Paris, des femmes, 1997), and Cixous's as yet unpublished play, *Rouen, la trentième nuit de mai 31* foregrounds themes of inspiration, memory and artistic responsibility within a multi-layered temporal structure. This play, initially about Joan of Arc was originally commissioned by Deborah Warner to be performed by Fiona Shaw. The project was not finalized and a rewritten version was read by Daniel Mesguich and an actor from the Théâtre de la Métaphore at the Cerisy conference in July 1998.

Of Altobiography

The contrast between two quotations, both from Hélène Cixous, is emblematic of the main question discussed in this article:[1]

Biographiquement, je pars, dès l'enfance, d'une révolte, d'un refus, immédiatement violent et angoissé d'accepter ce qui se passe sur la scène au bord de laquelle je me trouve déposée au terme d'une combinaison d'accidents de l'Histoire. J'ai eu cette étrange 'chance' : quelques coups de dés, une rencontre entre deux trajectoires de diaspora★, et au terme de ces chemins d'expulsion et de dispersion qui ponctuent, à travers les déplacements des juifs, le fonctionnement de l'Histoire occidentale je tombe – je nais – en plein sur une scène exemplaire un modèle nu, brut, de ce fonctionnement même : j'ai appris à lire, à écrire, à hurler, à vomir, en Algérie.
★Mon père, sépharade, – Espagne-Maroc-Algérie – ma mère askhenaze – Autriche-Hongrie-Tchécoslovaquie (son père) + Allemagne (sa mère) traversant par hasard un Paris éphémère...

(I come, biographically, from a rebellion, from a violent and anguished direct refusal to accept what is happening on the stage on whose edge I find I am placed, as a result of the combined accidents of History. I had this strange 'luck': a couple of rolls of the dice, a meeting between two trajectories of the diaspora,★ and, at the end of these routes of expulsion and dispersion that mark the functioning of western History through the displacements of Jews, I fall – I am born – right in the middle of a scene that is the perfect example, the naked model, the raw idea of this very process: I learned to read, to write, to scream, and to vomit in Algeria.
★My father, Sephardic – Spain-Morocco-Algeria – my mother, Ashkenazy – Austria-Hungary-Czechoslovakia (her father) and Germany (her mother) passing by chance through a Paris that was short-lived.)

Je ne redoute rien autant que l'autobiographie. L'autobiographie n'existe pas. Mais tant de gens croient que cela existe. Alors je déclare solennellement : l'autobiographie n'est qu'un genre littéraire. Ce n'est pas un genre vivant. C'est un genre jaloux, décepteur, – je le déteste. Quand je dis 'Je', ce n'est jamais le sujet d'une autobiographie, mon je est libre. Est le sujet de ma folie, de mes alarmes, de mon vertige.

(I dread nothing as much as autobiography. Autobiography does not exist. Yet so many people believe it exists. So here I solemnly declare: autobiography is only a literary genre. It is not a living genre. It is a jealous, deceitful sort of thing – I detest it. When I say 'I,' this I is never the subject of autobiography, my I is free. Is the subject of my madness, my alarms, my vertigo.)

The first of these extracts, taken from the essay *La Jeune Née* (*The Newly Born Woman*), is just one example of how powerful and all-pervasive the autobiographical dimension has been in Hélène Cixous's writing. Numerous other such examples can be found throughout her work over many decades in texts of a wide variety of genres. The permeation of other genres by the autobiographical is in itself neither a novel phenomenon nor a novel idea; it is now over twenty years since Paul de Man argued that 'any book with a readable title-page is, to some extent, autobiographical'.[4] What is so interesting in Cixous's case is the combination of the ubiquity of the autobiographical references and the resolute refusal, as vehemently expressed in the second quotation, of the genre of autobiography itself. This refusal is all the more marked given the number of genres with which Cixous has experimented.[5] For an author profoundly concerned with exploring – and displacing – generic limits, one might expect that autobiography, a genre whose limits are notably problematic, would have proven especially attractive. What, then, motivates her aversion to this particular form? And what are its implications for her *practice* of autobiography?[6]

In the interviews published in *Hélène Cixous, Photos de racines* (*Hélène Cixous, Rootprints*), Mireille Calle-Gruber suggests that what distinguishes Cixous's writing from autobiography is the fact that 'ledit "pacte autobiographique" qui codifie le genre est inopérant'[7] (the 'autobiographical pact' which codifies the genre is inoperative). In effect, the texts whose paratextual apparatus most clearly announces an autobiographical emphasis deploy a variety of strategies problematizing the identity between narrator and author that, according to Philippe Lejeune, institutes the pact leading the reader to class the text as an autobiography.[8] For example, the title of one section of *Jours de l'an* (*FirstDays of the Year*), 'Autoportraits d'une aveugle' ('Self-Portraits of a Blind Woman'), explicitly invokes the field of autoportraiture. But the narrator immediately differentiates between herself and the author: 'Pourquoi parlé-je de l'auteur comme si elle n'était pas moi? Parce qu'elle n'est pas moi'[9] (Why do I speak of the author as if she were not me? Because she isn't me). The use of the third person, combined with the attribution elsewhere in the book (92) of the name 'Hellia' (i.e. a name slightly different from 'Hélène') to the 'author', further emphasizes that the 'self-portraits' in question, instead of seeking to provide a mirror-image of the author, are an exploration of the self as Other, an attempt to paint the alterity of the self. Not *auto*, but *alto*biography.

In the section of *Photos de racines* entitled 'Albums et légendes' ('Albums and Legends'), the element of Cixous's published work to date which perhaps presents most clearly as an autobiographical venture, the narrator's identity is similarly uncertain. This short section, the only one in the book authored solely by Cixous, reproduces a number of photos from her family album, nearly all relating either to her mother's childhood or to her own, together with a commentary by Cixous on them. But at one point, when commenting on a photo of her grandfather's tomb in a deserted Russian forest, reproduced alongside a photo of her grandfather himself, the 'I' unexpectedly changes referent:

Photos: portals, porticos. I enter the forest. I have already seen trees. But neither I nor anyone has ever seen this grave. It is dead. Wooden letter, no one has come to hear you breathe. Standing, I copy the address onto the envelope: Hier ruht in Gott – Landsm. Michael Klein – II Komp L.I.R.G. – Gest. 27.7.16.

I copy and I cry.

Why these tears? Because I am dead. I am so dead. Because I have become this raised wooden stone that repeats my name and my date of death to the air where I never lived. The wooden page informs the empty wood that henceforth it is here that I live, become foreign earth and wood. Oh! I need God so as not to forget myself.

My name is Michael Klein. I am resting. I have lost my birth. How can one be so dead? The passer-by would teach me more than my death about myself. This is where I begin. The last day. But there are no passers-by. The entire forest has no address. Everything is interrupted.

The grass in disorder on my foot. To my left a Fritz, behind me a Paul behind Paul a... illegible behind Fritz a... illegible.

It happened thus:

Stopped short, cut, first the leg then the root. I am planted in a forest where no one I know has ever come to see me. All of a sudden, in July, I became Russian and dead. The shafts of the pine trees rise very straight among our crosses and our simple wooden stories. God is an unknown pine forest.

On the right, the standing soldier. To his left, preceding him in our reading which goes from left to right, his grave. But read from right to left according to the Hebrew mode, first him then his grave.[10]

By prosopopoeia, the 'I' becomes Michael Klein.[11] The 'I's foreignness to itself is further reflected in the striking use in French of a third person verb after a subject including the first person ('ni moi ni personne jamais ne l'*a* vue'), and especially in the strange sentence: 'De moi le passant m'apprendrait plus que ma mort' (The passer-by would teach me more than my death about myself). The English translation does not render the strangeness of the French 'de moi' which can also mean '*from* me': the passer-by would teach me what he would have learned *from* me (that I did not know I knew). A casual passer-by can in some sense learn more than oneself from oneself about oneself. A totally unknown Other can read me better than myself.

This passage is not merely of interest because it problematizes the referential relation between narrator and author which invites a text to be classified as 'autobiography'. It contains an implicit discourse on what writing the autobiographical more generally – i.e. non-generically – may mean for Hélène Cixous. In the French text, the metamorphosis of the 'I' can be read even before the assertion that 'my name is Michael Klein' in the masculine participle/adjective 'mort', dead: 'Parce que je suis *mort*' (Because I am dead). It is thus at the point describing her grandfather's transformation into a 'raised wooden stone' that the narrator herself changes persona; in the very act of rendering his death, she resuscitates him by eclipsing herself textually in his favour. By writing, she breathes new life into her unknown grandfather, enables him to reconnect with the birth the circumstances of his death had taken from him. 'First the leg then the root. I am *planted* in the forest': the intervention of the metaphor in effect *re*plants the grandfather, restores the connexion to his root, reverses the passage from the organic to the inorganic. Her 're-copying' thus transforms rather than reproduces. But of course by revisiting (in writing) the grandfather's tomb, by giving voice to the dead man's sense of abandonment at being buried far not only from family but from any 'passerby', Cixous is above all linking up with her own origins. Writing the autobiographical for her literally means giving voice to the unknown roots who make her what she is. Writing as *rerooting*.

Especially, this process is inseparable from a process of reading. Access to the resting-place of Michael Klein is possible only because a photo of the tomb exists: 'Photos: portals, porticos. I enter the forest.' The forest *in* the photo, but also the forest *of* the photo. From the beginning of the passage it is clear that looking at the photo involves a process of interpretation. Interpretation, moreover, of a specifically *written* trace.[12] The tomb with its inscription is described first as a 'wooden letter', subsequently as a 'wooden page' standing amid the (other) trees in an unknown forest, one with no 'address'. For Klein, it seems that the tragedy is less that he is dead, than that his new existence ('This is where I begin') as a dead man is cut off from any human contact, any interaction. 'Everything is interrupted.' Specifically, the text notes that the names of the soldiers in the background of the photo cannot be read: 'behind Paul a... illegible behind Fritz a... illegible.' But this very declaration of a break in relations paradoxically reminds the reader that Klein himself is being read; it is from the perspective of the viewer of the photo, not from that of the tomb within it, that the unknown soldiers' names are illegible. Reading, then, is what re-establishes contact with the grandfather – and what falsifies his assertion that 'everything is interrupted' even as he makes it. In retrospect we note that the possibility of this contact may date from the moment the narrator considers the photo. The narrator's entering the forest in/of the photo already opens a breach in the text, given that in the same paragraph the inscription on the tomb is declared a letter with an 'address'. Although the narrator cannot break her grandfather's isolation by 'reading' the photo, she can put it into circulation; the loss of address can itself acquire an address. Furthermore, her reading generates a virtuous circle to the extent that the grandfather's final declaration of his isolation, his cut-off status ('stopped short, *cut*'), takes place explicitly within the context of an address to the reader: 'It happened thus'. But whose reading of events is being proffered here, the grandfather's or the granddaughter's? Is the reader the granddaughter or the granddaughter's reader? Reading has in effect (re)established a circuit in which the reader is no longer clearly distinguishable from the read. The message of the passage as a whole is that renewing contact with one's roots is fundamentally a process of interpretation, of decipherment. We may note that the difference between 'a*l*tobiography' and 'a*u*tobiography' is, literally, *lu* (read). As the last paragraph quoted emphasizes, one's story of the past – as a move from life to death or from death to life – is: a matter of reading.

The focus on reading in this passage helps more generally to explain the title of the section of the book to which it belongs, 'Albums et légendes'. The Latin *legenda* means 'what is to be read'; by announcing the narrative of origins that is to follow as a collection of 'legends', the title not only calls into question its historical reality but emphasizes the role of reading both in its production and its reception. These 'legends' are readings *of* the past which in turn require reading. The text's incipit already brings this home forcefully:

Elles ont toujours été là.
Je ne les regarde pas. Ne les ai jamais regardées. Je les 'sais' là. Leur présence. Racines. Miennes? Mes si étrangères racines. (*Photos de racines*, 181)

(They have always been there.
I do not look at them. I have never looked at them. I 'know' they are there. Their presence. Roots. Mine? My so strange roots.) (*Rootprints*, 179)

The feminine pronoun 'elles', lost in translation, creates a link between the narrator's roots, feminine in French, and the photos, also feminine in French, which are evoked in the next paragraph and whose commentary will organize the text. Retrospectively, the roots turn out to be photos of roots, i.e. a version, or reading, of roots; the retrospective discovery itself highlights the process of reading in which the reader is currently engaged. The roots, inscribed in the third person, are the first subject of the text, 'étrangères,' strange, foreign: 'hers' only with a question mark. Her origins, far from offering a means to an illusory self-reunification, are radically inappropriable ('Je ne les regarde pas' can also mean 'I do not concern them', or 'they are unaffected by me'). Cixous's version of *Genesis* thus reads: in the beginning is the Other, accessible only via reading.

This 'autobiographical' section, focusing on photos of Cixous's origins, in turn seems to have determined the French title chosen for the book as a whole, *Hélène Cixous, Photos de racines*. Containing, in addition to 'Albums et légendes', not only the interviews with Calle-Gruber but also critical texts by Calle-Gruber and Derrida on Cixous, a text by Cixous on Derrida and selections from her notebooks, the book represents a reflection on Cixous's work in its entirety, not just some 'autobiographical' subset of it. This suggests that autobiographical writing, writing which seeks to explore one's origins or roots, is paradigmatic of 'writing' in general. Close to the end of 'Albums et légendes', Cixous herself stresses the link between the autobiographical and writing:

Ce que je raconte ici (oublis et omissions compris), c'est ce qui pour moi n'est pas dissociable de l'écriture. Il y a une continuité entre mes enfances, mes enfants, et le monde de l'écriture – ou du récit. (*Photos de racines*, 206)

(What I am recounting here (including what is forgotten and omitted) is what for me is indissociable from writing. There is a continuity between my childhoods, my children, and the world of writing – or of the narrative.) (*Rootprints*, 203-4)

The autobiographical is coextensive with writing, uncontainable within any generic limit. Cixous's distaste for 'autobiography' thus seems to relate not to the autobiographical enterprise *per se* but to the desire to impose a form on its expression – to contain the uncontainable – which subtends its codification as a genre. By insisting that her account is both voluntarily and involuntarily incomplete, she wards against the possibility of (mis)taking it for the totalizing narrative of a stable, unified self which was the conventional model of autobiography. The shift from 'écriture' to 'récit' in this quotation is eloquent, precisely because it introduces a generic distinction other than the autobiographical: Cixous differentiates, not between autobiographical and non-autobiographical texts, but between *narrative* texts and others. '*Ou du récit*': the final syntagm, detached from the body of the sentence by the dash, calls attention to itself, especially in relation to a writer in whose work a narrative drive has been conspicuously absent. As a reminder of Cixous's consistent rejection of all forms of narrative closure (including the kinds of narrative which became codified as autobiography), it functions as an autobiographeme, bearing out the sentence's assertion of the omnipresence of the autobiographical. But above all it acts as a warning that autobiographical narratives, like all others, are to be read as narratives. The choice of the word 'récit' towards the end of 'Albums et légendes' echoes its inscription in a short, untitled foreword or *avertissement* to the reader thrown into relief in the French version by being printed by itself on the double-spread following the section's title-page:

Toutes les biographies comme toutes les autobiographies comme tous les récits racontent une histoire à la place d'une autre histoire. (*Photos de racines*, 179)

(All biographies like all autobiographies like all narratives tell one story in place of another story.) (*Rootprints*, 178)

'Albums et légendes' is thus framed by a cautionary reminder that the account it contains of Cixous's history should not be constructed as a privileged source of truth because the author is also the object. 'Autobiography' is just one narrative among others, telling one story among others. 'Une histoire': everything in the text combines to stress that the 'history' being recounted is one of a number of possible 'stories'. For example, it runs counter to traditional models of autobiography by giving priority from the outset to space rather than time, without, however, replacing a totalizing history with an equally totalizing geography. The map of Europe which is the text's initial illustration (its first 'photo') is read over many pages in such a way as to situate the narrator not in a unified space but at the intersection of spaces (as does this article's opening quotation). Furthermore, mingled spaces mingle with mingled times:

Ce qui constitue le sol originaire, le pays natal de mon écriture est une vaste étendue de temps et terres où se déroule ma longue, ma double enfance. J'ai une enfance à deux mémoires. Ma propre enfance a été accompagnée et illustrée par l'enfance de ma mère. (*Photos de racines*, 183)

(What constitutes the originary earth, the native country of my writing is a vast expanse of time and lands where my long, my double childhood unfolds. I have a childhood with two memories. My own childhood was accompanied and illustrated by the childhood of my mother.) (*Rootprints*, 181)

Even the narrator's childhood is not wholly 'hers'! The 'native country' of her writing is: mingling. Her childhood memories mingle with memories of her mother's childhood, suggesting that memories and memories of – her mother's? – memories are equally valid – or invalid – as readings of the past.

The promised 'histoire' turns out to be a geography; the emphasis on its textual – i.e. fictional – nature suggests that the writer, no less than the reader, does not know in advance which version of her story she will tell; *what* is being told depends on *how* it is told, on how the writing brings it into being.[13] By adopting such strategies guarding against the institution of a 'referential pact',[14] Cixous renders the classification of the text highly problematical. In other words, even in 'Albums et légendes', the text which to date approximates most closely to an 'autobiography', Cixous's autobiographical practice, far from investing in redefining the genre, resists generic codification. That is why I call it *alto*biography: not a 'new' form of autobiography, but something differently autobiographical, autobiography's other.[15]

The unexpected foregrounding of narrative in 'Albums et légendes' may also help to shed light on how the autobiographical references function in Cixous's less overtly autobiographical texts. For the opening quotation is typical of the Cixousian autobiographeme in that it remains surprisingly close to the classic, narrative autobiographical model. In effect, references in Cixous's works to the author's life regularly focus on its chronological development. Her parents' histories, her passionate attachment to her mother in infancy, her father's death while she was still a child: these are just some of the 'events' which reappear systematically, insistently throughout her oeuvre. Astonishing as it might appear for a writer whose fiction (especially the early texts) has been to the fore in inventing new forms giving precedence to a non-totalizing discourse over narrative – forms analogous in many respects to those evolved 'in' autobiography by innovators such as Barthes and Valéry[16] – the autobiographical for Cixous remains closely bound up with narrative.

Cixous's use of narrative, however, in no way consolidates the notion of a unified, historical self which the narrative would seek to reanimate. On the contrary, as we saw, her roots were 'étrangères' (foreign) from the beginning: her origins were *originarily* other. Similarly, far from charting the chronological development of a subject coinciding perfectly with itself, the events which compose the 'story' of her life are markers of a fundamentally dynamic subjectivity, an ongoing process of alteration within the self. Her text explores – reads – events as precipitators or catalysts of a fracture in subjectivity, but in a subjectivity always already divided. Rather than positing an undivided self to whom events happen, she is interested in the self *to whom events give rise*. Indeed, her hostility to autobiography seems partly explained by the fact that for her the term apparently excludes the (uncertain) narrative of such a(n uncertain) self: 'Il peut y avoir ces fractures du moi passionnantes que sont les confessions. Ce sont pour moi des oeuvres, des livres. Appelons cela autobiographie, mais c'est une version. C'est la version de l'aveugle' (*Photos de racines*, 96) (There can be those intriguing fractures of the self that are called confessions. For me these are works, books. We can call this autobiography, but it's one version. The blind person's version) (*Rootprints*, 87). The 'version' of autobiography she finds compatible is the one written in the dark, venturing into the unknown regions of the self. Moreover, if 'confessions' represent 'des oeuvres, des livres' (works, books), it is presumably because they display the extent to which they constitute a reworking of reality rather than a would-be *copie conforme*. The only version of autobiography she values is thus the one recognizable precisely as a version of events.

A narrative pattern can be detected in Cixous's writing in which the key characteristic is that the events the narrator relates are those which happen to her, those over which she has no control. This is true of the opening extract where we saw her birth strikingly described in terms of a roll of the dice: 'J'ai eu cette étrange 'chance': quelques coups de dés (...) je tombe, – je nais – (...) en Algérie' (I had this strange 'luck': a couple of rolls of the dice (...) I fall – I am born – (...) in Algeria.) The role of chance as author of the events narrated is a key leitmotiv in her writing; in 'La Venue à l'écriture' ('Coming to Writing'), a chess metaphor intensifies the impression of the narrator's being totally at a loss to predict (and thus prepare for) the autobiographical event most privileged in Cixous's works, her father's death:

Le visage primitif a été celui de ma mère. Sa face pouvait à volonté me donner la vue, la vie, me les retirer. A cause de la passion pour le premier visage, j'ai longtemps attendu la mort de ce côté. Je gardais ma mère à vue, avec la férocité d'une bête. Mauvais calcul. Sur l'échiquier, je couvais la dame; et c'est le roi qui est tombé.[17]

(The primitive face was my mother's. At will her face could give me sight, life, or take them away from me. In my passion for the first face, I had long awaited death in that corner. With the ferocity of a beast, I kept my mother within my sight. Bad move. On the chessboard I brooded over the queen; and it was the king who was taken.)

The sense of the narrator being utterly exceeded by events is reflected on a grammatical level in the 'I''s disappearance at the end of the quotation (after three instances in quick succession where it figured as active subject: 'j'ai longtemps attendu (...) Je gardais (...) je couvais'). The narration of the same event in *Jours de l'an* features even more strongly the narrator's eviction from the place of subject, inscribing her emphatically first as indirect object and then in the passive mode:

Le douze février, à moi, est arrivé ce qui n'arrive qu'une fois et à une seule personne sur terre ce jour-là, à moi à qui aucune date n'était jamais arrivée, aucune flèche, pas une, le douze février 1948, c'est à cette date que j'ai été mise en douze, le monde a sauté comme un seul soldat sur une mine, il a été déchiqueté, le monde dans lequel j'avais été conçue et j'avais cru que j'y demeurerais. (*Jours de l'An*, 65-6)

(On February twelfth happened – to me – what only happens once and to one person on earth that day, to me to whom no other date had ever happened, no arrow, not one, February twelfth, 1948, on this date I was broken in twelve, the world exploded like a single soldier on a mine, it was torn to shreds, the world in which I had been conceived and had believed I would dwell) (*FirstDays*, 43; translation modified)

The inversion of subject and verb initially suggesting the absence of *any* subject accompanying the verb 'arriver' powerfully reflects the bereft child's sense of overwhelming disruption; the disintegration of her world is echoed in the division of what would more usually compose one paragraph in two. The alinea marks the difference between the narrator's identity before that date – although its apparent unity is already problematized by the repetition of 'à moi' – and afterwards; *she* is 'mise en douze' (cut in twelve) on the fateful twelfth. However, the repetition of the verb 'arriver', a recurrent signifier in Cixous's work, highlights its double meaning of 'to happen' and 'to arrive', indicating that the disintegration has a positive as well as a destructive side.

Events thus figure as an otherness reaching her, whose effects on her *as* subject then often become the main subject of the text. A succinct example can be seen in the following short extract from a lecture, doubly autobiographical in that the autobiographical element Cixous introduces into her discussion of other texts is an account of the autobiographical origin of her writing: 'The first book I wrote rose from my father's tomb. (...) I wouldn't have had death, if my father had lived. I have written this several times: he gave me death. To start with'.[18] Within the space of a few lines, the narration of the 'event' – in this case, the origin of her writing – is immediately followed by an analysis of its significance.[19] The same text later illustrates how Cixous's concern in reworking her life in writing is always to interpret it for herself:

I lived in Clos Salembier, in the upper outskirts of Algiers, and to get to school everyday I passed (I went by bus, the K line) in front of the Catholic cemetery. The Catholic cemetery was my death as a Jewish girl. The cemetery spoke Latin. It said to me: *o mors, spes et victoria.* I heard *le mors* (*the horse's bit*), *l'espèce* (*the species*); a horse resisted, who(se) was (the) victory? Everything happened to me in the cemetery, in a hostile manner. ('School of the Dead', 8)[20]

As a child, Cixous was already reading/deciphering her life; writing the text, she is literally *re*reading it. While the text from 'The cemetery spoke Latin...' to '...victory?' follows the child's perspective, the preceding and subsequent sentences analyse the event from an adult point of view. This fragment is particularly interesting because the event whose meaning for her Cixous is spelling out is not only – in contrast with the positive way Cixous generally evokes the plurilinguism of her childhood environment[21] – a hostile encounter with another language, ecclesiastical Latin, the language of the (Catholic) other; it also represents the advent of language *as* other. But the humour of the discrepancy between the Latin inscription and the child's translation of it brings out above all Cixous's *enjoyment* of the otherness of language, her relation to it as ally, as resource, not as weapon. She has often stated that this acute sensitivity to language, dating back to childhood, was a key determinant in her turning to writing. As this passage shows, the difference between child and adult lies in the latter's greater ability to read the traces the chance events of her life have left.

Cixous, then, uses narrative as a means not of self-(dis)closure but of self-discovery. Like the 'confessions' she esteems, her autobiographical writing is a study of herself as a version of herself, an exploration of the other she very nearly did not become, the other that by chance she *is*. Commenting elsewhere on the difference between a focus on subjectivity and individualism, she affirms: 'When I explore I – I take as object of observation a human sample'.[22] She explores herself as she would explore an other, as the singular example of humanity that she – like everybody else – represents. But whom – like everybody else – she can access only through reading. As the premium placed on the signifier throughout Cixous's work makes impossible to ignore, her text offers no more and no less than *a version of a version of herself*. Let us recall that the first words of the opening quotation in this article are: 'Biographiquement, je pars', literally, 'biographically, I leave'. In effect, Cixous's writing *starts from* the biographical: events in the author's life function as a springboard, a point of departure which she leaves behind in writing – in order to discover in writing. It is in writing that their significance emerges. The events Cixous 'happens' to write about are precisely those which happen to her *in* writing, that is, those which writing enables her to read.

MAIREAD HANRAHAN
University College Dublin

NOTES

1 I would like to thank Johnnie Gratton and Susan Marson for their comments on a first draft of this article.
2 Hélène Cixous and Catherine Clément, *La Jeune Née* (Paris, 10/18, 1975), pp. 127-8; *The Newly Born Woman*, translated by Betsy Wing (Minneapolis, University of Minnesota Press, 1986), p. 70.
3 Hélène Cixous, *Le Livre de Promethea* (Paris, Gallimard, 1983), p. 28; *The Book of Promethea*, translated and with an introduction by Betsy Wing (Lincoln and London, University of Nebraska Press, 1991), p. 19; translation modified.
4 'Autobiography as De-facement', *Modern Language Notes* 94 (1979), 922. The autobiographical element of fiction in particular gained currency considerably earlier. In one of the earliest contributions to the theory of autobiography, Georges Gusdorf pronounced that 'every novel is an autobiography by intermediary' ('Conditions and Limits of Autobiography', reprinted in *Autobiography: Essays Theoretical and Critical*, edited by James Olney (Princeton, Princeton University Press, 1980), p. 46).
5 The 'By the same author' list in *Osnabrück*, Cixous's latest book at the time of writing this article, includes fiction, essays, criticism, theatre, short stories and a 'nouvelle poétique'.
6 There has been little consideration of Cixous's relationship to autobiography. One exception is Mary E. Schipa, 'Hélène Cixous: Sur la piste d'une

autobiographie féministe', *Romance Review* 5:1 (1995), 29-37; Susan Sellers, *Hélène Cixous, Authorship, Autobiography and Love* (Cambridge, Polity Press, 1996) does not address this issue, despite the mention of 'autobiography' in the title.
7 Mireille Calle-Gruber and Hélène Cixous, *Hélène Cixous, Photos de racines* (Paris, des femmes, 1994), p. 95; *Hélène Cixous, Rootprints* (London and New York, Routledge, 1997), p. 86.
8 Philippe Lejeune, *Le Pacte autobiographique* (Paris, Seuil, 1975).
9 Hélène Cixous, *Jours de l'an* (Paris, des femmes, 1990), p. 153; *FirstDays of the Year*, translated and with a Preface by Catherine A.F. MacGillivray (Minneapolis and London: University of Minnesota Press, 1998), p. 101.
10 'Photos: portes, portiques. J'entre dans la forêt. J'ai déjà vu des arbres. Mais cette tombe, ni moi ni personne jamais ne l'a vue. Elle est morte. Lettre de bois, personne n'est venue t'entendre respirer. Je recopie l'adresse sur l'enveloppe debout: Hier ruht in Gott – Landsm. Michael Klein – II Komp L.I.R.G. – Gest. 27.7.16.

Je recopie et je pleure.

Pourquoi ce pleur? Parce que je suis mort. Je suis si mort. Parce que je suis devenu cette pierre de bois levée qui répète mon nom et ma date de mort à l'air où je ne vécus jamais. La page de bois prévient le vide bois que c'est ici que désormais je demeure, devenu terre et bois étranger. Oh! j'ai besoin de Dieu pour ne pas m'oublier.

Je m'appelle Michael Klein. Je me repose. J'ai perdu ma naissance. Comment peut-on être si mort? De moi le passant m'apprendrait plus que ma mort. C'est ici que je commence. Le dernier jour. Mais il n'y a pas de passant. La forêt tout entière est sans adresse. Tout est interrompu.

Les herbes en désordre sur mon pied. A ma gauche un Fritz, derrière moi un Paul derrière Paul un... illisible derrière Fritz un... illisible.

Cela s'est passé ainsi:

Arrêté net, coupé, d'abord la jambe ensuite la racine. Je suis planté dans la forêt où personne de connaissance n'est jamais venue me voir. Tout d'un coup, en juillet, je suis devenu russe et mort. Les hampes des pins montent très droit parmi nos croix et nos simples histoires de bois. Dieu est une forêt de pins inconnue.

A droite, le soldat debout. A sa gauche, le précédant dans notre lecture qui va de gauche à droite, sa tombe. Mais lue de droite à gauche selon le mode hébreu, d'abord lui ensuite sa tombe.' (*Photos de Racines*, p. 189; *Rootprints*, p. 186).
11 He in turn becomes first a stone and then, by virtue of the metaphorical 'planted', a tree: far from being clearly distinguishable from each other, animal, mineral and vegetable are forms of existence which overlap, resisting rather than promoting neat categorization.
12 The continuation of the passage considers the visual aspect of the photo, describing it as an 'abstract portrait' of the grandfather himself.

13 In his discussion of 'Savoir', a short text by Cixous on the 'loss' of her myopia due to a successful laser operation, Jacques Derrida points out that the recounting of the same event produces a different text in *Messie*: 'On pourrait ainsi tenir tel passage de *Messie* (des femmes, 1996, pp. 142 *sq.*) pour une traduction poétique de *Savoir*. A moins que ce ne soit l'inverse. C'est une autre version, un autre poème, infiniment différent et jumeau cependant, presque contemporain, par l'opération, par le "miracle" et par le deuil qu'il nomme' (Hélène Cixous and Jacques Derrida, *Voiles* (Paris, Galilée, 1998), p. 56) (A passage in *Messie* (des femmes, 1996, pp. 142 *sq.*) could thus be considered a poetic translation of *Savoir*. Or vice versa. It's another version, another poem, infinitely different and yet its twin, nearly contemporary by virtue of the operation, the "miracle" and the mourning it names).
14 *Le Pacte autobiographique*, p. 36.
15 Here is where I differ from Mary E. Schipa who examines *Hélène Cixous, Photos de racines* as 'une éventuelle redéfinition féministe du genre' (a possible feminist redefinition of the genre). See *art. cit.*, 32.
16 See Paul L. Jay, 'Being in the Text: Autobiography and the Problem of the Subject', *Modern Language Notes* 97:5 (1982), 1045-63.
17 Hélène Cixous, 'La Venue à l'écriture', in *Entre l'écriture* (Paris, des femmes, 1986), p. 11; 'Coming to Writing,' in '*Coming to Writing' and Other Essays*, edited by Deborah Jenson; translated by Sarah Cornell, Deborah Jenson, Ann Liddle, Susan Sellers (Cambridge MA and London, Harvard University Press, 1991), p. 3.
18 Hélène Cixous, 'The School of the Dead,' in *Three Steps on the Ladder of Writing*, translated by Sarah Cornell and Susan Sellers (New York, Columbia University Press, 1993), p. 12; unpublished in French.
19 Space permitting, I would argue that a similar pattern is increasingly perceptible at a macrostructural level in Cixous's work. For example, an autobiographical event (the discovery of a box of letters written by her father to her mother during their engagement) proves a springboard in *OR, les lettres de mon père* (Paris, des femmes, 1997) for the narrator not only to reflect on how different she might have been had she read the letters decades earlier, but also to take stock of the other she has become by virtue of having had the author of those letters for her father.
20 For the overdetermination of the 'K line', see *Jours de l'an*, pp. 66-8 (*FirstDays of the Year*, pp. 43-4). 'K' has also been a dominant letter in other texts, notably those referring to Freud's *Dora* case or to Kafka's writings.
21 See for example *Photos de racines*, p. 183, *Rootprints*, p. 182; 'La Venue à l'écriture,' p. 31, 'Coming to Writing,' p. 21; 'My Algeriance', in *Stigmata: Escaping Texts* (London, Routledge, 1998), p. 168.
22 Hélène Cixous, 'Preface', in *The Hélène Cixous Reader*, edited by Susan Sellers (London, Routledge, 1994), p. xvii.

Agony or Ecstasy? Reading Cixous's Recent Fiction

Since Cixous's work was first published over thirty years ago, her fiction has always met with extreme reactions. Readers either love it or hate it. It all depends, it seems, on whether her complex, poetical writing speaks to you, or not. At one end of the spectrum, aficionados celebrate her work with their own Cixousian readings of Cixous's texts; at the other, her writing is met with accusations of elitism, utopianism, her polysemic fiction just too difficult, too demanding of the reader, untranslatable, unteachable, even unreadable.[1] This polarity in the responses to Cixous's work deserves further examination, especially given the implications of her polemical feminist-oriented essays of the 1970s which argue for the liberating and transformative power of literature: reading and the reader (thus Cixous's own readers) must be significant players in the processes of socio-political and psychological change that she envisages, although her small readership and the marginal status of her work means that the impact of her own writing will be limited. In the first instance, this article considers how and why Cixous's fiction continues to provoke such extreme reactions; it then goes on to engage more specifically with the idea that literature can bring about change by exploring the nature of the interaction between text and reader in Cixous's work through an analysis of *Beethoven à jamais ou l'existence de Dieu*.[2]

The terms, agony and ecstasy, of my title relate only in part to the extreme responses Cixous's work elicits; rather, their etymology provides the broader framework for my discussion of reading. 'Agony', meaning pain or anguish, also carries the sense of struggle from the Greek *agon*, a contest. Here, the relationship between Cixous's texts and the reader is considered in terms of *agon*, by highlighting some of the factors which operate on the reading of her work. The second term, 'ecstasy', signifies rapture. Its Greek root, *ekstasis*, literally means standing outside – beyond one's normal state of mind or self. In this respect, I consider what Cixous's fiction can give to the reader, arguing that s/he is encouraged to go beyond (as in *ekstasis*) – beyond the text, beyond the text/reader *agon*, beyond even the self (in the senses of thinking differently as well as ecstasy).[3]

Most post-Barthesian reading theory points to a two-way interaction between text and reader with both the text and the reader as sites of plurality. Reading is thus in a sense a 'cross-fertilisation' of what is in the text with what the individual reader brings to his or her reading; the reader acts as co-creator of the text, an active partner in meaning production.[4] According to this framework, the reader is conceptualized as powerful but not completely free since the text itself to some extent always directs his or her interpretation, even if that direction is ultimately open-ended, as I argue in the case of Cixous's fiction. Among the various paradigms of interactive reading proposed by contemporary reading theorists, Lynne Pearce's model of the dialogue is most suitable to this particular dynamic of text/reader relations, conceptualizing reading not only in democratic and reciprocal terms, but also as taking place within a framework of power relations – or here, *agon* – between text and reader: a politics of reading.[5] The reader invoked in this article is similar to Iser's concept of the 'implied reader', which, itself an effect of interpretation, enables the relationship between text and reader to be discussed in terms of the interaction between textual strategies and the act of interpretation, while, at the same time, allowing for differences between individual readers.[6]

Throughout Cixous's prolific and varied oeuvre, the presence of the/an author is unfailingly inscribed. The author-figure is a seductive figure, and indeed, for texts to have the transformative effect that Cixous champions, they first have to seduce their readers.[7] Notably, it is not the seductiveness, or otherwise, of the real-life woman (Cixous) that is relevant here, but instead, the figure of the, or an, author which is made present within the body of the text. Nonetheless, the differentiation between the two is not always clear-cut. On the one hand, the blurred boundaries between fiction, theory and autobiography in Cixous's work, and the fact that the Cixousian narrator is nearly always also a writer writing, do inscribe a version of Cixous herself as an ever-present author-figure into her texts. On the other hand, the actual identity of this textual author-figure is always kept uncertain, unstable and ultimately unknowable. Thus, although Cixous's first-person narrator is not to be simply equated with Cixous herself, neither can she be fully separated from her.

As I have argued elsewhere in the context of gender and reading, the presence of an author-figure in Cixous's fiction in such textual practices as direct reader address is both controlling and generous,[8] but its effects are not necessarily only applicable to gender-specific modes of reading. Although Cixous's early fictions were addressed to an indisputably female reader (addressed as a feminine 'you' or 'we'), a supposedly inclusive strategy but which in practice is of course alienating to many individual women readers, all Cixous's more recent fictions since the pivotal *Le Livre de Promethea* (*The Book of Promethea*), have constructed readers (*lecteurs*) as both male and female.[9] One effect of direct address is to draw the reader into the text. In *Jours de l'an* (*FirstDays of the Year*), as indeed in much of Cixous's fiction, direct address includes the reader in the process of writing: 'Je vais vous faire un aveu: depuis dix jours j'essaie d'écrire une dernière page pour ce livre' (I'm going to make you an avowal: for ten days I've been trying to write a last page for this book).[10] Here, the narrator/writing subject confides in the reader, sharing her difficulties with writing the text. Reader address is of course a positioning device, but in Cixous's work there is often a generous outcome. At the end of *Jours de l'an*, the book which is being written throughout the duration of the text is left unfinished to fly away with 'un grand bruit d'ailes' (276) (the loud sound of wings) (187), undoubtedly released to its readers to contribute their part in its creation. A similar relinquishing of the text by the 'author' to her readers takes place at the end of both Cixous's *L'Ange au secret* and *Le Livre de Promethea*.

The author-figure is also made present by the self-referential character of Cixous's work. Fiction and theoretical texts are interdependent, echoing each other in terms of themes, analyses and, even, identical passages: 'Il y a une façon de dire tulipe qui tue toute tulipe. Il y a une façon clarice de faire-tulipe, et de la tige jusqu'aux prunelles je vois comme la tulipe est vraie'[11] (There is a way of saying 'tulip' that kills every tulip (*tue toute tulipe*). There is a Clarice way of making-the-tulip, and from the stem to the eye's pupils, I see how the tulip is real). Exactly the same words appear, in the original French, in both the essay 'L'Approche de Clarice Lispector' and the fiction text *Illa*. Indeed, since Cixous so readily and frequently identifies herself in both essays and fiction with the Brazilian writer Clarice Lispector, the multitude of references to Lispector in Cixous's work also contributes to its self-referentiality. Cixous's essays offer useful insights into her fiction (and vice versa), but this can be as limiting as it is illuminating if it means that they are read principally from one particular (authoritative) perspective: her own theoretical framework.

If the self-referential character of Cixous's work means that her reader is contained within the Cixous corpus, sent from one Cixous text to another and back again, the heavily intertextual nature of her writing is much more open-ended, leading the reader out from the Cixousian oeuvre to an array of literature and art from a wide range of cultures. This positive effect must, however, be offset against the anxiety intertextuality can induce in the reader. Indeed, many of the problems that readers seem to experience with Cixous's writing are partly due to the wealth of intertextual references which make it both so rich and so dense.[12] Julia Kristeva, theorizing the phenomenon of intertextuality and like Cixous, the revolutionary potential of literature, speaks of all texts as being under the 'jurisdiction' of other texts.[13] Kristeva's choice of terminology introduces the notion of a conflict or *agon* that is always already within the fabric of the text itself, and this conflict engenders a similar one between text and reader. Cixous's *L'Ange au secret* is saturated with a vast array of references to authors and literary texts, from Homer, Virgil, Dante and Shakespeare to Poe, Dostoyevsky, Kafka, Bachmann, Bernhard and Lispector. For Cixous's readers, this is more than just literary name-dropping; such blatant intertextuality must always have repercussions on the politics of reading. So wide a spectrum of references can be experienced as a sort of textual terrorism, inducing anxiety and alienation in readers whose own reading histories do not necessarily include the same set of authors or texts, and yet who, by means of these very references are made to feel that their knowledge of them is assumed.

Cixous's intertextuality does, however, also work in a more generous way, particularly in cases where references are extended and elaborated in order to illustrate a particular point. In *L'Ange au secret*, references to other literary texts combine with strategies such as direct reader address to involve the reader in a discussion of crime and guilt, with the association, over several sections of the text, of Dostoyevsky's *The Devils* with Poe's 'The Murders in the rue Morgue', both of which portray death occurring behind closed doors.[14] Cixous's narrator explicitly emulates the narrative style employed in Poe's short-story to draw her reader along in a re-evaluation of the crime of the rape of a young girl to which Dostoyevsky's character, Stavrogin, confesses. Pointing to a narrative gap in Stavrogin's confession, she suggests that the girl's own desire for him makes her unrapeable; in actual fact his real crime is far worse, far worse even than the bestial murders of Poe's tale – that of subsequently and knowingly driving the girl to suicide. This point forms the basis of a self-reflective sequence in which the narrator, once again by direct address ('Et vous?' (133) (And what about you?)), encourages the readers to examine their own consciences. Although a greater sense of inclusion is to be experienced by readers who are familiar with both *The Devils* and 'The Murders in the rue Morgue', in this particular instance, extended discussion, clear references and sufficient commentary are given not to alienate the uninitiated reader. Indeed, such forms of intertextuality are generous, leading the readers not only out of the text they are reading by offering opportunities for further reading and (re)interpretation, but also within themselves, in this instance to prompt ongoing reflection about ethical issues.

Cixous's poetical writing style is a strong element in the politics of reading. The sensuality, rhythm and language games of her writing strengthen other effects which involve the reader in the text. In *Déluge*, the reader is drawn into the text by means of the narrator's meditation on the inadequacy of language to describe the nuances and subtleties of the feelings she is trying to convey:

Il fait si sombre ici où je cherche une langue qui ne fait pas de bruit pour chuchoter ce qui n'est ni vivant ni mort. Tous les mots sont trop forts, trop rapides, trop assurés, je cherche les noms des ombres entre les mots, comment s'appellent les choses qui restent,
        Comment s'appelle l'amour qui reste après l'amour
        Je t'aime n'est pas vrai, je ne t'aime pas est faux. (111)

(It is so dark here where I seek a language that makes no sound to whisper what is neither living nor dead. All the words are too loud, too fast, too sure of themselves, I am searching for the names of the shadows between the words, what to call the things that are left,
        What is the love called which remains after love has gone
        I love you is not right, I do not love you is wrong.)

In addition to being programmed to reflect on the limitations of words, here the reader is sensitized to the poetical possibilities of the language used to describe its own inadequacies. Paradoxically, in this lamentation of a lack of appropriate words, the liberating potential of language is brought to the fore as the inexpressible ('the shadows between the words') is in this very way actually, poetically, expressed.

Cixous's poetical writing is seductive and this can be as controlling as it is generous; the confiding nature of the last example positions its readers to share the narrator's viewpoint as well as offering them the pleasures and possibilities of the aesthetics of the writing. Elsewhere in *Déluge*, the use of rhythm seems designed to draw the readers in and hold them within the text:

Et toujours se demandant qui tue qui, qui m'a tuée, qui tué-je, qui tues-tu toi qui me tues qui frappes-tu en moi, et moi qui en toi désiré-je soit abattre en pleine poitrine soit égorger qui désiré-je mordre au sang qui cracher, qui jeter par la fenêtre, et toi qui en moi enterres-tu vivante, qui veux-tu déporter, recouvrir de tonnes de temps, et moi qui foudroyer du regard qui agenouiller qui (203–4)

(And always wondering who kills who, who killed me, who did I kill, who do you kill you who kill me who do you strike in me, and me who in you do I desire either to strike right in the heart or to slit their throat who do I desire to bite and draw blood who to spit out, who to throw from the window, and you who in me do you bury alive, who do you want to exile, to cover up with tons of time, and me who to look daggers at who to bow down who)

Although in translation the impact of the alliteration between *tu* (you) and *tue* (kill) of the French original is lost, the intensity of the passage is still felt in its rhythm. The paragraph ends without punctuation in mid-sentence. The following paragraph of the text continues the interrupted sentence without an initial capital letter, and this format is sustained for two pages. Each unfinished paragraph draws the reader onto the next. The breaks are like pauses for breath, a coming up for air, before the text plunges once again into the maelstrom of self-reflection it evokes, including the readers by direct address and holding them within it, to encourage, or even lead them into a similar meditative mode. In reality, the effects of reading are not of course as predictable as this, and alternatively, this very intensity might have the opposite effect – that of alienating the reader.

Déluge is an account of a woman's abandon by her lover, but it also relates to abandonment in a more universal way, involving the reader by means of slippages from a first person singular narrative to an unspecified, general 'we':

Nous ne savons pas ce que trahir-et-abandonner veut dire. La trahison dans la nature humaine est infinie. Nous ne pouvons même pas imaginer le millionième de nos trahisons. De nos sentiments de trahisons. La trahison nous trahit. Nous trahisonne.
    Nous-même nous nous trahissons dix fois, cent fois par jour, nous nous ôtons nous-même le pain de la bouche, nous laissons tomber dans l'escalier l'enfant que nous avons sauvé du feu. Je ne nous comprendrai jamais. L'amour nous échappe, la nature humaine nous échappe. Heureusement. Loin de nous
                               la trahison trahit. (159)

(We don't know what betray-and-abandon mean. Betrayal is infinite in human nature. We can't begin to imagine one millionth of our betrayals. Of our feelings of betrayal. Betrayal betrays us. We betray.[15]
    We betray our own selves ten times, a hundred times a day, we take the bread out of our own mouths, we let the child we rescued from the fire fall down the stairs. I will never understand us. Love escapes us, human nature escapes us. Thank goodness. Far from us
                               betrayal betrays)

In this extract, 'we' overtly refers to humanity as a whole but the effect of its repetition and of the incantational quality of the passage is to reinforce the inclusion of the individual reader: everyone is capable of hurting and being hurt; we, ourselves, hurt and are hurt; I personally, hurt and am hurt. The indentation of the last line breaks the rhythm and focuses attention on the slippage of the final words. Although we as individuals may be complicit with humanity's failings, this does not mean those failings are necessarily part of our own character. It is possible for us, personally, to live differently and, by the way we act, to resist those failings. In this way, readers are led by the text into themselves to reflect beyond the relationship portrayed in the text, on relationships in general, and especially, on their own. This is perhaps one of the most seductive and generous aspects of reading Cixous's fiction: the poetical evocation of internal, emotional reality makes the slippage from her non-realist texts to the lived reality of the reader an easy, even an inevitable passage. In this sense, Cixous's fictions are about ourselves, but far from making the unacceptable assumption that everyone thinks and feels like her narrative figures, this is to say instead that the passage between text and reality is an open-ended and individual one, allowing each reader his or her own pathway. Cixous's readers are always constructed as active; plenty of space is allowed for the reader's imagination, and multiple interpretations are made possible by means of the uncertainty inscribed in the fabric of the text: ambiguous language and genre, uncertain chronology and narrative voice, slippages between figures, between time, between narrative levels, between dream and reality, between inside and outside, between text and life.

The aforegoing analysis of the politics of reading Cixous's fiction suggests that the same textual factors have different (even opposite) effects. In practice, the features I have highlighted – the interdependence of Cixous's theory and fiction, her intertextuality and self-referentiality, the author-figure, reader address, linguistic and syntactical play – the very factors which draw some readers in are just as likely to alienate others, which might account for some of the polarity of responses to her work. So far, I have suggested that the most generous effects of Cixous's fiction take the form of encouraging open-ended interpretation, and of leading the reader out of the text. The emphasis has, however, been on textual strategies and markers rather than on reader interpretation *per se*. As a counter-balance, and in order to evaluate the transformative potential of Cixous's fiction, the final part of this article shows how *Beethoven à jamais ou l'existence de Dieu* opens up to its readers real possibilities of liberation from imprisoning stereotypes of representation and from the aggression of binary thinking. In her essay, 'Le Sexe ou la tête?' ('Castration or Decapitation?'), Cixous identifies the need to work on three different aspects of 'the couple' in order to make progress towards socio-cultural change: first, the couple in binary thinking (the relation of one polarized term to another); second, the male/female couple (the gendered political relation of domination/subordination in phallogocentric culture); and third, the individual couple (the personal and loving relationship of one person with an/other).[16] *Beethoven à jamais ou l'existence de Dieu* addresses all three.

In this text, which explores the creative potential of love, constant slippage between the figures of an un-named, contemporary male/female couple and a couple from history, Beethoven and his lover (the Immortal Beloved) renders the borders between the personal and the universal indistinct. Cixous's Beethoven both is and is not the composer Beethoven, functioning rather as a symbol of an artist dedicated to his work as well as the figure of an individual man. Above all, Beethoven provides Cixous, who has often spoken about her inability to create male characters, with a ready-made desiring male figure for this text about love.[17] Beethoven might, however, appear to be a rather surprising choice since, although he was evidently a fascinating man, he is renowned for being unable to commit himself to a lasting emotional relationship.[18] Within the text, Cixous's narrator chooses Beethoven as an exemplary character for the story she tells, on the one hand, because his writing – his music, his self-reflective diary and his letters, among which a now famous love letter to the unknown 'Immortal Beloved' – suggests and provides a way of writing about love, and on the other, because he is a 'feminine' man. In *La Jeune Née*, Cixous suggests that artists (men and women) have to open themselves up to sexual differences within themselves in order to create.[19] In this way, as 'un homme si largement environné de musique' (76) (a man so considerably surrounded by music), a musician and artistic creator, Cixous's Beethoven figure is a 'feminine' man – different, unusual, inexplicable:

Mais dans cette histoire, l'homme pourrait tout aussi bien être une femme, pensons-nous, et simultanément nous pensons pourtant cet être-là est un homme en tout. C'est, dans la région du coeur, une hypersensibilité, une source d'alerte, au sein du feu, le point de lait. (131)

(But in this story, the man could just as easily be a woman, we think, and simultaneously we think, but that person is a man in every way. It is, something emotional, a kind of hypersensitivity, an intuitiveness, in the bosom of passion, the place where the milk flows)

He has qualities which are so often, and stereotypically, associated with women (sensitivity, intuition, passion, maternity), and yet he is also very much what is considered to be a 'real man'.

If the real Beethoven's actual words of love exist, in his now-published love letter, few of them appear in Cixous's text. Instead, she uses his 'style haletant' (70) (breathless style): the way his love letter, and indeed most of his correspondence, is punctuated by dashes.[20] In *Beethoven à jamais ou l'existence de Dieu*, the section entitled 'Lettre à l'immortelle bien-aimée' (Letter to the Immortal Beloved) is written in this way, with dashes between phrases and sentences, but the words are the narrator's (and Cixous's) interpretation (fictionalization) of the passion and emotion with which the composer wrote his love-letter. Rather than his actual words, Cixous's fictional version is an interpretation of Beethoven's 'voice', in the sense of the Kristevan semiotic, or indeed of the Cixousian 'feminine' – the emotion of the voice being detectable in the interstices of the sentences he wrote. The love affair between Beethoven and his Immortal Beloved, epitomized in and by his love-letter, is echoed by, interweaves with, and slips between that of the contemporary couple – 'her' and 'him'. The lack of consistent differentiation between the two couples means it is not always possible to tell whether the pronoun 'he', the initial 'B', or even the name Beethoven, relate to the figure of Beethoven himself or to the contemporary man. The unnamed couple therefore also figure more conceptually as a couple in love (any couple in love, arguably even, at times, all couples in love).[21]

Their love story is, however, no conventional tragic or fleeting romance. *Beethoven à jamais ou l'existence de Dieu* is concerned with the possibilities of a lasting passion, at once evoking and differentiating itself from such great tragic romances as Tristan and Isolde, as well as from the trite clichés of much contemporary romance. The 'God' (*Dieu*) of the title makes reference to the transcendental and immortal dimension of both love and artistic creation, which enables us to experience extreme heights of emotion. Artistic inspiration frequently takes on mystical qualities in Cixous's work.[22] In *Beethoven à jamais ou l'existence de Dieu*, love too is mystical; falling in love is magical. In the text, and in life, 'God' is invoked at moments of intense passion; perhaps, Cixous's narrator goes as far as to suggest, both the word and the concept 'God' exist because of the need to give expression to such moments. Despite references to external reality (a cafe, streets, traffic, telephones, planes), *Beethoven à jamais ou l'existence de Dieu*, in common with all Cixous's fiction, is primarily concerned with feelings and emotions, and with the importance of writing. We know of Beethoven's relationship with his Immortal Beloved only because of the love letter he wrote – an ode, and as it turns out, an attestation to the immortality of his love. In Cixous's text, diaries, notebooks, letters (real and potential), songs and narrative express the emotions of a love affair: the intensity of life, fear of loss, joy, hurt, togetherness and separation, the implications of becoming a couple.

Following *Déluge*, which is concerned with the pain of loving and hurting, Cixous turns in *Beethoven à jamais ou l'existence de Dieu* to the close analysis of some positive, creative aspects of relationships. Beethoven's 'feminine' (different) voice is present in the promises the man makes to the woman, promises which are part of the (self-)construction of the couple and of their creativity. Two of these promises warrant particular attention: 'Je te serai toujours infidèle, comme à moi-même' (71-2) (I shall always be unfaithful to you as I am to myself) and 'Je ne t'épouserai jamais' (82) (I shall never marry you). The first, 'I shall always be unfaithful to you as I am to myself' is of course a confession but a promise is implicitly contained within it. Music is what comes first in the man's life (in Beethoven's life) and it always will, but that does not mean he will betray his beloved. On the contrary, by means of this promise, he puts her on an equal footing with himself. To forget himself (his own needs) for his music is not to betray himself; rather, it is to be true to himself. And so, 'A l'infini, fidèle et infidèle se rejoignaient aussi' (72) (In infinity, fidelity and infidelity were also at one). Here the binary opposition between fidelity and infidelity is dissolved, the relations between the terms changed, and productively, creatively, although perhaps only momentarily, fidelity is contained within infidelity. When Cixous's Beethoven declares his infidelity, he is trusting his beloved with a part of himself, and paradoxically he is pledging that he will be faithful to her.

The second promise, 'I shall never marry you', is followed by several pages of meditative and interrogative narrative introspection, in which the phrase is examined, explored and discussed by the narrator, on behalf of, and with, not only the woman in the text but also Cixous's readers. The phrase perplexes because it is not an answer to a question. There has been no question. It is a free-floating statement, but between the words and meaning is the man's voice, its tone, its inflections, giving meaning to the words which are spoken. It is the man's voice and his intonation, saying 'never' as if he were saying 'always', insisting that this phrase is interpreted as a promise and not a warning. Cixous's readers are not however left to find this interpretation for themselves; it is made abundantly clear in the text:

Toujours – (…) toujours – je ne t'épouserai pas – et jamais je ne t'aurais épousée – et à la fin – jamais – si tu veux bien – je ne t'aurai épousée –

tu m'entends – je t'entends, oui – je veux bien – et je m'entends avec toi t'écouter – goutte à goutte – j'écoute chaque goutte tomber suivie – tu me suis – oui je te suis – goutte à goutte – et ensuite j'écoute le *à* qui respire d'une goutte à l'autre – les sons entre les mots je les écoute et là où il n'y a pas de son pour faire la liaison – j'écoute le silence qui célèbre le temps – (87)

(Always – (…) always – I shall not marry you – and never would I have married you – and in the end – never – if you'd like – I would not have married you –

you hear me – yes, I hear you – I'd like to – and I hear myself with you listening to you – drop by drop – I listen to each drop falling followed – you follow me – yes I follow you – drop by drop – and then I listen to the sound between one drop and another – the sounds between the words I listen to them and where there is no sound – I listen to the silence celebrating time –)

Here, as in Cixous's next fiction text, *La Fiancée juive de la tentation*, conventional marriage and its vows are rejected in favour of the greater commitment of a pledge or promise between lovers.[23] *Beethoven à jamais ou l'existence de Dieu* ends on a performative, creative note, as the couple say 'Jetaime' (235) (Iloveyou). The words are run together; the phrase is a cliché. It is clear, however, that this couple have dispensed with the empty, automatic promises that so often go with conventional declarations of love. Their promises, and the phrase 'Iloveyou', are meaningful in the context of their own relationship. Clichés are shattered and re-formulated differently.

In both cases, a particular interpretation of the promise is given in the text, and thus we might wonder whether any creative space remains for the reader. Is this just another example of the controlling nature of Cixous's writing? Of course, not all readers will be seduced by Cixous's play between language and meaning here. However, the very non-conventionality of the promises and, in particular, the long process of reflection connected with the latter one would seem actually to provide readers with food for thinking differently. Rather than reducing the interpretive opportunities, the open-ended nature of Cixous's writing encourages her readers to reflect creatively about language, about meaning, about promises, about relationships, about their own relationships. *Beethoven à jamais ou l'existence de Dieu* is worked through with elements of creativity – music, writing, interpretation, fiction, poetical language and love all figure in the text itself – and this, together with the usual prevalence of Cixousian textual slippages, encourages readers to read creatively, in the interstices between historical periods, between narratives, between figures, between language and meaning, between imagination and reality, and between the text and real life. The problems that Cixous's couple encounter in *Beethoven à jamais ou l'existence de Dieu* are not the stuff of far-fetched fantasy, nor are their solutions utopian; rather, they readily find echoes in the ordinary but often painful reality of many people's lives. Moreover, since the real subject of *Beethoven à jamais ou l'existence de Dieu* is love itself, I would go so far as to suggest that the questions it raises about how we love one another and the individual creativity that love can produce may even be relevant beyond the boundaries of the heterosexual configuration of the couples within the text.

The between-ness that is created in *Beethoven à jamais ou l'existence de Dieu* encourages a dialogue between text and reader on a different dimension – in *extasis* – beyond the limitations of ordinary language and the enclosure of binary thinking. The textual space is a creative space of individual negotiation for the reader, who is led beyond the text, beyond even the constraints of his or her own life, to recognize that realities of difference are actually to be found within the self, and that the potential of those realities can be realized in his or her own lived relationships. Cixous's fiction will no doubt continue to be beset with conflicting reactions and a minority status, but this does not necessarily negate its transformative impact. Individual interventions of difference into the social order can eventually make a difference on a larger scale.

To analyse Cixous's fiction through a politics of reading is admittedly rather a brutal way of looking at such nuanced poetical writing but, as this article shows, the model of a dialogue for reading does include the provision of a response to aesthetics – to voice, tone, inflection, stress. The reader may to some extent be controlled, seduced (although not always successfully), but in Cixous's case this control, seduction, is ultimately generous, since it can engage the reader in an interaction with the text well beyond the moment of reading. To read Cixous positively is perhaps to be a complicit partner to her textual seductions but it is never to be a passive one. Far from only offering utopian visions, her recent fiction opens up spaces in both internal and external reality, within the self and in relations with others, which, while offering food for thought, do not deny the force of either socio-cultural expectations or the individual power relations that operate on personal relationships in reality. Cixous's fictions may be difficult but the effort involved in reading them is productive. They lead the reader to think anew but they do not necessarily prescribe set alternatives; rather, they make the reader do the work, fostering a productive and creative interaction between text and life, initiating a reading dialogue which is not only agonistically (agonizingly) political but also out/standingly (ecstatically) meaningful.

GILL RYE
Institute of Romance Studies (University of London)
and
University of Surrey Roehampton

NOTES

1 See, for example, Susan Sellers, *Hélène Cixous: Authorship, Autobiography and Love* (Cambridge, Polity Press, 1996) for a reading of Cixous's fiction which explicitly follows Cixous's own reading practice; examples of extreme negative reactions to Cixous's body of work tend to be oral rather than written, but see Véronique Hublot and David Douyère, 'Il faut lire Hélène Cixous...', *Entre Deux* 2 (1995), unpaginated.
2 Hélène Cixous, *Beethoven à jamais ou l'existence de Dieu* (Paris, des femmes, 1993).
3 With thanks to Armand d'Angour for his advice.
4 *Intertextuality: Theories and Practices*, edited by Michael Worton and Judith Still (Manchester, Manchester University Press, 1990) p. 1. For interactive models of reading relevant to my argument here, see Ross Chambers, *Room for Maneuver: Reading (the) Oppositional (in) Narrative* (London, The University of Chicago Press, 1991); Lynne Pearce, *Feminism and the Politics of Reading* (London and New York, Arnold, 1997); Michael Riffaterre, *Text Production*, translated by Terese Lyons (New York, Columbia University Press, 1983); Emma Wilson, *Sexuality and the Reading Encounter: Identity and Desire in Proust, Duras, Tournier and Cixous* (Oxford, Clarendon Press, 1996).
5 Lynne Pearce, *Reading Dialogics* (London, Edward Arnold, 1994).
6 Wolfgang Iser, *The Implied Reader: Patterns of Communication in Prose Fiction from Bunyan to Beckett* (London, The Johns Hopkins University Press, 1974). My reader is, however, more active than Iser's is usually conceptualized to be.
7 The etymology of the term 'seduce' is illuminating here: *se-ducere* = to lead aside. Seduction is controlling but can also be theorized as generous, especially when it relates to the intellectual seduction which applies to reading. See Ross Chambers, 'Alter Ego: Intertextuality, Irony and the Politics of Reading', in *Intertextuality: Theories and Practices*, pp. 143-58, for an analysis of textual seduction.
8 See Gill Rye, 'Weaving the Reader into the Text: The Authority and Generosity of Modern Women Writers', *Women in French Studies* (1997), 161-72.
9 Hélène Cixous, *Le Livre de Promethea* (Paris, Gallimard, 1983); *The Book of Promethea*, translated by Betsy Wing (Lincoln and London, University of Nebraska Press, 1991).

10 Hélène Cixous, *Jours de l'an* (Paris, des femmes, 1990), p. 274; *FirstDays of the Year*, translated by Catherine A.F. MacGillivray (Minneapolis and London: University of Minnesota Press, 1998), p. 186. Translations of all quotations from Cixous's *L'Ange au secret* (Paris, des femmes, 1991), *Déluge* (Paris, des femmes, 1992) and *Beethoven à jamais ou l'existence de Dieu* are by Kath Massam and Gill Rye.

11 Hélène Cixous, 'L'Approche de Clarice Lispector'; Se laisser lire (par) Clarice Lispector; A Paixao Segundo C.L.', in *Entre l'écriture* (Paris, des femmes, 1986), pp. 115-38 (p. 131); *Illa* (Paris, des femmes, 1980), pp. 155-6. 'Clarice Lispector: The Approach; Letting Oneself (be) Read (by) Clarice Lispector; The Passion According to C.L.', in *Coming to Writing and Other Essays*, edited by Deborah Jenson (Cambridge, Mass. and London, Harvard University Press, 1991), pp. 59-77 (p. 72).

12 See Michael Riffaterre, 'La Trace de l'intertexte', *La Pensée*, 215 (October 1980), 4-18, which argues, on the reader's behalf, that recognition of intertextual references is not necessary but the presupposition that they exist is.

13 Julia Kristeva, *La Révolution du langage poétique: L'Avant-garde à la fin du XIXe. siècle: Lautréamont et Mallarmé* (Paris, Editions du Seuil, 1974), p. 339.

14 Fyodor Dostoyevsky, *The Devils (The Possessed)* (Harmondsworth, Penguin, 1971); Edgar Allan Poe, 'The Murders in the rue Morgue', in *The Works of Edgar Allan Poe*, 10 vols (London, Lawrence & Bullen, 1895) III, pp. 53-98.

15 'Nous trahisonne'. This ungrammaticality contains play with sound and gender which the English translation cannot do justice to.

16 Hélène Cixous, 'Le Sexe ou la tête', *Les Cahiers du GRIF* 13 (October 1976), 5-15; 'Castration or Decapitation?', translated by Annette Kuhn, *Signs* 7:1 (Autumn 1981), 41-55.

17 See for example, 'Conversations', in *Writing Differences: Readings from the Seminar of Hélène Cixous*, edited by Susan Sellers (Milton Keynes: Open University Press, 1988), pp. 141-54 (p. 151).

18 See Maynard Solomon, *Beethoven* (London, Cassell, 1978), p. 157. Beethoven's total dedication to his music seems to have precluded any long-term close relationships.

19 Hélène Cixous and Catherine Clément, *La Jeune Née* (Paris: 10/18 Union Générale d'Editions, 1975), p. 153; *The Newly Born Woman*, translated by Betsy Wing (London: I.B. Tauris, 1996), p. 84.

20 A translation of the 'Letter to the Immortal Beloved' is reproduced in Solomon's *Beethoven*, pp. 159-60. See also *Ludwig van Beethovens Sämtliche Briefe*, edited by Emerich Kaftner (Tutzing, Hans Schneider, 1975), for facsimiles of some original letters.

21 In this way, *Beethoven à jamais ou l'existence de Dieu* develops similar themes and techniques to Hélène Cixous, *Manne aux Mandelstams aux Mandelas* (Paris: des femmes, 1988).

22 The term 'God' is ambiguous in Cixous's fiction, since sometimes it is used literally and sometimes metaphorically, and indeed this very ambiguity is exploited. In the body of the text of *Beethoven à jamais ou l'existence de Dieu*, the word is most often spelt without a capital letter. The title itself is ambiguous, since in all instances in the book, the whole of the title is spelt in capital letters. Frequently, the term 'God' in Cixous's work relates to artistic inspiration and also to writing itself. See Catherine Clément, 'Cixous la sauvage', *Magazine littéraire* 280 (September 1990), 76-7, for a discussion of Cixous's mysticism and the god-figures in her fiction.
23 Hélène Cixous, *La Fiancée juive de la tentation* (Paris, des femmes, 1995).

The Ethics of Rewriting the Loss of Exile in *Manne aux Mandelstams aux Mandelas*

Sans un témoin comment mourir notre mort comment souffrir notre souffrance?[1]
(Without a witness, how to die our death how to suffer our suffering?)

Où chercher le témoin pour lequel il n'est pas de témoin?[2]
(Where to look for the witness for whom there is no witness?)

To conceive of bearing witness to an event that destroys its only witness is to envisage performing an impossible act. Yet in this reading of Hélène Cixous's *Manne aux Mandelstams aux Mandelas* (*Manna for the Mandelstams for the Mandelas*) I want to explore the performance of just such an impossibility. *Manne* is framed as an attempt to approach experiences that the writing self will never be able to claim as her own: the exile, torture, and solitary death of the Russian poet Osip Mandelstam, the condemnation to imprisonment of Nelson Mandela, and the experiences that the women in their lives undergo in trying to come to terms with their separation and loss. The ethical wager for the writing self in this text is how to write about these experiences without making them her own; she must bear witness to her own disappearance in order to give a voice to the specificity of the other. The ethics of such a self-effacing gesture appear laudable and it is possible to trace a flickering rather than a stable presence of the narrating 'je' in *Manne* as she moves from the foreground to the background of the lives of the Mandelas and the Mandelstams. However, what I want to argue here is that this flickering presence of the narrating 'je' presents us with a deftly constructed loss of self that preserves the centrality of the very position it seeks ethically to marginalize.

Manne is a poetic elaboration of select historical facts from the lives of Osip and Nadezhda Mandelstam and Nelson and Winnie Mandela leading up to the time of the text's publication in 1988. Throughout the text, the writing self is concerned to specify differences between herself, the Mandelas, and the Mandelstams, and the ethical impulse of Cixous's writing of difference in *Manne* is everywhere apparent. An openness to the other – in particular, the sexually different other – is an important facet of Cixous's work in her early writings on 'écriture féminine', the ethical thrust of which takes us through to the writings on theatrical production that Cixous deems to be the culmination of her approach to all kinds of others. By reworking the relation between Cixous's *Manne*, her writings on 'écriture féminine' and on the theatre, I want firstly to emphasize necessary differences between *Manne* and these other writings, differences that constitute the specificity of her ostensibly ethical approach to others in this text. But this focus on the specific difference of *Manne* will lead me to the rather thornier ethical issue that I wish to explore secondly. One of the many strands that link the narratives of the Mandelstams and the Mandelas is the experience of exile that both couples undergo. While the 'je' of *Manne* is indeed dealing with experiences of exile that are alien to her, she also presents us with an uncanny repetition of familiar Cixousian themes, and this leaves us with an equivocal view of Cixousian openness to others. Exile emerges elsewhere in Cixous's writing as the condition of possibility for writing as such, and the affirmative reworking that exile undergoes in *Manne* proves to be less attentive to differences between the self and historical others than we may be led initially to expect. Although the writing self of *Manne* bears witness to the impossibility of stepping into the position of the other, it will become apparent here that this is because she has been in that position all along.

Cixous's decision in *Manne* to bring out parallels and intersections between the lives of the Mandelas and the Mandelstams and to work them into one narrative is, as Morag Shiach has pointed out, a risky endeavour. The danger, as Shiach sees it, lies in the potential loss of difference between the Mandelstams and the Mandelas to the point where the acts of writing poetry and engaging in guerrilla warfare become almost indistinguishable at times.[3] Shiach's reading serves importantly to draw attention to elisions of difference within this text, and my own reading will attend ultimately to a loss of difference between the writing self and her subject matter. Yet I wish to begin here by highlighting the ways in which differences between the various positions *are* maintained in *Manne* even as those positions are made to overlap.

In a Cixousian textual space, a writing that animates rather than annuls differences within and between self and other could perhaps fittingly be labelled 'écriture féminine' after Cixous's description of this practice in 'Le Rire de la Méduse' ('The Laugh of the Medusa'). Indeed, Susan Sellers's reading of *Manne* makes precisely this connexion, understanding *Manne* explicitly as a powerful evocation of 'écriture féminine'.[4] While I too wish to indicate the ways in which *Manne* could be classified as an instance of writing in the feminine, my own analysis of this text differs significantly from that of Sellers. I want to use the designation of 'écriture féminine' as a starting point rather than an end-point for describing the writing of difference that we read in *Manne*, since there is an attempt in this text to negotiate ways of approaching differences other than sexual difference alone. While the interwoven narratives of exile focus on relations of sexual difference, they also bring out other differences within and between the identities of this text.

The Russian poet Osip Mandelstam, arrested in 1934 for writing a satirical poem about Stalin, underwent brutal interrogation before being sent to spend a three-year period of exile in Voronezh. He died in captivity after being re-arrested in 1938 and sentenced to five years in a labour camp. Nadezhda went with her husband into exile and she – along with Winnie Mandela – becomes one of the sustaining forces of life and love in Cixous's text. Winnie and Nelson's story is a love story that we join a long time prior to Nelson's condemnation in 1964 to a life of exile. (*Manne* was published two years prior to Mandela's release in 1990 and eight years prior to Winnie and Nelson's divorce in 1996). But the day of the trial, along with the entry into exile, looms large from the outset. In the interview 'A propos de *Manne*' Cixous states that it was Winnie who inspired her to write about (the) Mandela(s): the power that this woman exercised over Cixous when she saw her for the first time on television captured the writer's imagination.[5] In Cixous's subsequent play 'Voile noire, voile blanche/Black sail, White sail', which reworks some of the material from the Russian component of *Manne*, Nadezhda Mandelstam features as one of the central figures in an all-female cast, reinforcing retrospectively Cixous's interest in the women in the intersecting narratives of *Manne*.[6] Although the women of *Manne* are in many ways the drive behind the text and the life-force that sustains the men, the positions of the protagonists are by no means fixed rigidly according to the division of sexual difference. In keeping with Cixous's earlier writings on a feminine economy, both the men and the women of this text are capable of being open to the other (sex) and 'écriture féminine' seems initially to accommodate the writing of (sexual) difference at work here.

Cixous's celebration of a writing that affirms rather than denies the feminine in 'Le Rire de la Méduse' is encapsulated in her definition of the other bisexuality as the 'repérage en soi, individuellement, de la présence, diversement manifeste et insistante selon chaque un ou une, des deux sexes'[7] (each one's location in self of the presence – variously manifest and insistent according to each person, male or female – of both sexes). This ability to sustain the other (sex) within the self is deemed to be a feminine capacity open to both men and women. The lengthy opening dedication to the ostrich in *Manne* introduces sexual difference in terms of parity between the sexes, even as it gestures towards the blurring of boundaries between the male and the female. But by encouraging us to think differently about the associations this flightless bird has with putting its head in the sand and hiding from situations rather than facing up to them, the text opens on a note that urges us to face up to numerous injustices and not just to those pertaining to sexual difference.

Associated with sexual equality because both the male and the female watch over the eggs and the offspring, the ostrich, which is gendered feminine in French, also comes to symbolize the male heroes of this text. Significantly, the term 'autruche' contains the other – 'autre' – in French. The flightless bird serves appropriately to ground the ensuing narrative in terms of a forgotten sacrifice: 'Ce livre voudrait être une déclaration d'amour à l'autruche oubliée, à la donneuse de feu et à tous les donneurs de feu qui payent de leurs ailes pour que les humains voient un peu plus clair dans le noir.' (*Manne*, 13) (This book would like to be a declaration of love to the forgotten ostrich, to this fire-giver and to all the fire-givers who pay with their wings so that human beings can see a bit more clearly in the dark) (*Manna*, 6). The text implores us to remember this sacrifice by giving back to these fire-givers (Mandelstam, Mandela, and the ostrich) in fiction what has been taken away from them in reality: the freedom once again to fly and to know no boundaries. Such freedom can only be restored in the fictional realm, but in order for the fictional (re)writing of the sacrificed other's experience to take place, the writing self must face the issue of how to write about that which falls far beyond the realm of her own experience. This necessitates reckoning with differences that stretch far beyond the realm of sexual difference alone.

The attempt at compassion in *Manne* involves an admission of the writer's limitations in gaining access to the specific experiences of the Mandelas and the Mandelstams. This is evidenced clearly at one point in the opening section of the text in which 'je' negotiates a tentative relation to Mandela and then to Mandelstam. With reference to Mandela, and acknowledging that she is writing from one side of the colour-divide responsible for the existence of apartheid, 'je' asks: 'Comment vais-je oser parler d'un noir destin moi dont le destin en apparence est blanc?' (22) (How shall I dare to speak of a black destiny, me, whose destiny is apparently white?) (13). The question of sexual difference, although an issue in relating to the male other, is not what concerns her here. The writing self is asking with what right she can write about what she will never experience because of being born one colour and not another. She acknowledges her (racial) difference from the other by admitting the impossibility of experiencing and of being able to bear witness to events she nonetheless wishes to recount: 'je veux assister à ce dont je ne suis pas le témoin' (24) (I want to be present at that to which I'm not a witness) (14). The admission of this impossible desire leads her to the scene of Osip Mandelstam's death – along with a recognition here of her having to negotiate an even more painful difference from herself. Once again, we move into a more complex sphere of differences between self and other that can only add to the attendant tribulations that may otherwise be associated with approaching the sexually different other.

Reiterating her earlier statement that the book she is writing is an attempt at compassion, she emphasizes that it is *only* an attempt, since she will never know what it feels like to go through what Mandelstam has been through: 'Seules les supplications me passent par le cœur. J'entends et ne sens pas, je pleure et ne saigne pas' (25) (Only the supplications pass through my heart. I hear and do not feel, I weep and do not bleed) (15). The writing self cannot know the physical experience of torture in the flesh, and, in this sense, the distance between the writing self and the victim is radical. The radical split between self and other indicated here in relation to Mandelstam, and elsewhere, in relation to Mandela, testifies to the difficulty of only exploring this text as an example of writing in the feminine. In its relative silence about differences other than sexual difference, Cixous's definition of the other bisexuality within a feminine economy raises the question as to whether the label, 'écriture féminine', when applied to the more expansive field of differences negotiated in *Manne*, is perhaps too restrictive if it goes without qualification. In responding to a text in which the writing self is not only approaching the lives of those she is writing about as a woman, it seems rather limiting to locate self-other relations solely within the parameters of a discourse on sexual difference. It is important not to lose sight of the issues of sexual difference that are obviously still crucial to Cixous's writing project here, but they do not remain the sole focus of her interest. While *Manne* moves beyond the openness to sexual difference *alone* designated by 'écriture féminine', it does not move beyond an openness to sexual difference *per se*.

I want to pause momentarily here and refer back to the aforementioned quotation and its assertion of a radical difference between self and other. For according to the writing self of *Manne*, what cannot be known in the flesh can be approached compassionately through the heart. This statement, acknowledging what passes by way of the writer's heart, evokes Cixous's description in a later essay of how writing for the theatre helped her to open out to others. If we look to Cixous's writing on her work for the theatre, we see that the heart is the realm in which differences of all kinds are united without indifference. Following the trajectory of Cixous's writing career that she herself describes in 'De la scène de l'Inconscient à la scène de l'Histoire', many commentators have emphasized the link between *Manne* and Cixous's theatrical writings.[8] Theatrical production emerges, in Cixous's view, as the logical development of an ethical approach to writing that seeks perpetually to question how the writing self can relate better to others. *Manne* marks a notable return on Cixous's part to writing poetic-fiction after a period of writing for the theatre and it is possible to read the text as the fictional-poetic culmination of the lessons Cixous learned in the theatre. While such a connexion seems unavoidable, I want nonetheless to mark a distinction between *Manne* and Cixous's writing for the theatre and this involves reading Cixous against herself.

Although the theatrical space has been present in the Cixousian oeuvre from her 1971 play *La Pupille* onwards, the essay 'De la scène de l'Inconscient' describes the theatre as the culmination rather than the starting point of an ethics of writing. In this essay the question that Cixous states that she feels able to address in the theatre is that of how to write (on) others without dominating them or exchanging their voices for her own. Writing for the theatre transforms the writer's ego into a space in which the other can appear. While the writing of fictions is a more obviously 'self-centred' activity, theatre enables Cixous apparently to attain a state of 'démoïsation' (an emptying of the ego or a dispossession of the writing self) in which the writer literally becomes the stage upon which others appear. Thus, theatre, for Cixous, is the gateway to approaching and writing about others who had not featured previously in her fictional writings. She states that she is able to write parts for historical characters and with this passage to the writing of historical others comes the question of writing parts for men – an issue Cixous claims she had not felt able fully to negotiate previously. The work of representing sexual difference in theatre is done by the actors' bodies rather than by the writing itself: they furnish the parts that Cixous is unable to provide herself. When Cixous returns to the fictional realm in *Manne* after the apprenticeship she claims to have served at the theatre, her writing, as we have already seen, becomes the space in which the sexually different/historical other can speak his/her difference from the writing self.

In *Manne* the historical others – both male and female – speak in the first person and it could thus be claimed that an ethical fading of the writing self – akin to that which happens in the theatre – has occurred in order to let these others speak. However, this reading of Cixous's fiction in terms of her theatrical production risks losing sight of an important difference between the two kinds of writing. This difference can be demonstrated paradoxically by turning to the very realm in which these two kinds of writing seemingly overlap: the realm of the human heart.

In 'De la scène de l'Inconscient', Cixous describes her theatrical characters as being born from the chest. The heart is the realm in which differences no longer divide: 'J'ai vu que les racines humaines ne connaissent pas les frontières et que (...) tout en bas de l'escalier du monde, il y avait le cœur'[9] (I saw that human roots know no borders and that (...) at the very bottom of the ladder of the world, the heart was beating). When writing for the theatre, the aforementioned 'démoïsation' is the state that Cixous feels the writer must achieve, and this happens in conjunction with the actors. Yet if this state is transposed onto the writing of fictions, I would argue that it becomes rather more problematic than it is enabling for an ethics of writing.

If the writing self disappears in fiction and becomes the stage for the other, there is no way of telling the difference between whether the writer has sacrificed herself to the other or whether there has been a colonization of the other by the self, or vice versa. In 'De la scène de l'Inconscient', we get an implicit, quasi-Levinasian acknowledgement of the other's priority over the self, but if these two positions become one, then this is problematic in ethical terms. One voice – even if it is seemingly the voice of the other – is not enough to indicate an openness to difference. If the self is to be open to the other, the direction of flow between the two positions and the acknowledgement of openness has to be laid bare. Although the common ground symbolized by the heart is to be found in Cixous's fiction as well as in her theatre, it is where differences between the writing self and the other are (re)instated – rather than elided – that Cixous's ethical approach to the other in fiction becomes apparent. The shifting narrative point of view in *Manne* allows us to envisage just such an approach precisely since it prevents us from seeing this text as the fictional-poetic illustration of Cixous's ostensibly ethical theatrical performances. Contrary to reading *Manne* in line with Cixous's pronouncements in 'De la scène de l'Inconscient', then, it is only by reading her against herself that we glimpse the ethical impulse in her approach to the other in her fiction.

In the opening sections of the text, the writing self gets closest to the figure of Winnie Mandela, who is referred to more frequently than not by her African name, Zami. In this opening section, 'je' states that she is literally inhabited by Zami. Zami is described as entering and leaving the writing self until she settles at a given moment within the writer: 'c'est alors que je lui ai cédé toute la place de mon âme et elle est entrée à jamais sans aucun mal et comme si elle était chez elle' (*Manne*, 20) (it was then that I ceded her all the space in my soul and she entered forever without harm and as though she were at home) (*Manna*, 11). In spite of this definitive admission of Zami's presence in the writing self, 'je' does not speak as Zami throughout the text, even though Zami's point of view features frequently. This intermittent presence of Zami as 'je' never stabilizes fully and finally, as the varied strategies of narration make clear.

Later in the text, it is Zami who is subject to being entered by an other (Nelson), but the narrative voice enacts a shift in positions that opens the voice of the writing self once again to Zami. Thinking back to when she fell over when running along the Bizana path at the age of four and saw herself bleed for what presumably was the first time, Zami is spoken about and then speaks as follows: 'Ce fut sa première peur de l'autre qu'elle était. Zami a regardé son genou. C'est par là, a-t-elle pensé, que Nelson a commencé à m'arriver, il y a longtemps (…). Il y a encore la cicatrice. Pour que tu entres, mon amour' (64) (This was her first fear of the other that was she. Zami looked at her knee. This is how, she thought, Nelson began to come to me, a long time ago (…). The scar is still there. For you to enter, my love) (44). Zami is spoken about in the third person, before having her thoughts reported and then, finally, addressing her loved one directly. In this final direct address there is little doubt that Zami is speaking, but the shift in point of view is just one instance of a blurring in the fictional realm between the voice of the writing self and that of the other (Zami, here). This blurring and shifting of narrative point of view happens frequently throughout the text as all the figures in the narrative speak in the first person at some point, causing us at times to question who precisely is talking, the writing self or these others. Yet we are never left in doubt for long as to the identity of the speaker, which is usually established retrospectively. While it would be a problem in ethical terms if we were to be left permanently puzzled as to who is speaking, this momentary lack of clarity brings the writing self closer to these others but ultimately reinstates the boundaries necessary for the recognition of difference and specificity.

Although the boundaries between the theatrical writing self and her characters must necessarily be lost, then, it seems crucial for Cixous's ethics of fictional writing that only a temporary loss of distinction between self and other takes place. A loss of difference between the positions in this text could be read as the height of generosity and self-sacrifice to the other but it could always also be read as a colonization of the other by the self or vice versa. We have observed that Cixous's shifting narrative points of view prevent any ultimate loss of distinction between the writing self and her characters in *Manne*. With this necessary preservation of difference between positions in mind, the writing self of *Manne* may appear to gain access ethically to what she can never experience herself without colonizing the position of the other or allowing her own position to be lost. But it is arguable that the preservation of difference between positions that is an ethical necessity here is sustained in all senses throughout the text.

Although the writing self approaches the Mandelas and the Mandelstams with a view to allowing their experiences to be narrated as their own, these experiences are not as unique to these protagonists as they initially appear. The fact that the exiles experienced in *Manne* are described in such a way as to overcome separation and loss affirmatively takes us back to a Cixousian concern that is not specific to the Mandelas and the Mandelstams alone, but rather pervades Cixous's oeuvre from the outset. The question we need to pose, with this affirmative reworking of exile and loss in mind, is whether the writing self is able ethically to rework somebody else's experience of exile (and of death in the case of Mandelstam) in line with her positive way of thinking. Is the writing self able to rewrite the loss of exile without erasing the fact that others, in *Manne*, may experience this state differently? Responding to this question, I would argue that the ethics of *Manne* are cleverly staged but that they constitute what, in Levinasian terms, might be called 'le jeu du Même'[10] (the play of the same): a form of writing that others the writing self rather than opening out to a position that is wholly other. In order to see how this occurs, we need to look firstly at Cixous's notion of exile.

Cixous understands exile in a positive sense. She states in the essay 'Difficult Joys': 'Exile – real or imaginary exile – presides over the destiny of writers.'[11] Far from perceiving the state of exile in which the writer lives as an irredeemably tragic condition, Cixous sees it as 'a source of creation and of symbolic wealth' ('Difficult Joys', 13). Thus, where we might think we hear echoes of Julia Kristeva when Cixous asserts that exile is a precondition for writing, Cixous is in fact saying something quite different. Kristeva asserts: 'Rien ne s'écrit sans quelque exil'[12] (Writing is impossible without some kind of exile), but for Kristeva exile is bound up with a melancholic state that accompanies an inability to accept separation and loss. Cixous's exile is a happy state, and this distinguishes her clearly from Kristeva; yet in another sense Cixous is perhaps closer to Kristeva's work on exile than this divergence suggests.

Taking up Freud's notion of the uncanny in her work on exile and estrangement, Kristeva thinks about unfamiliar otherness in terms of that which was once familiar to the self. As she explains elsewhere when talking about the uncanny: 'the Freudian message, to simplify things, consists in saying that the other is in me.'[13] In Levinasian terms, this relation between self and other is nothing other than the unethical 'play of the same', since the self here contains the otherness that Levinas would locate in a separate sphere. It is via these (unethical) workings of the uncanny, though, that Cixous and Kristeva might be brought together. For in reworking the association between exile, separation, and loss in *Manne*, Cixous renders the Mandelstams's and Mandelas's unfamiliar experience of exile in wholly familiar terms. The experience of the other turns out to be a very subtle distortion and uncanny repetition of the self-same.

Manne ends with the assertion: 'Et rien n'aura jamais été perdu' (342) (And nothing will have been lost) (254). Yet this can only be affirmed by a text that testifies to the loss of everything: 'Qui ne perd pas ce qu'il a, n'a pas ce qu'il a' (250) (Whoever doesn't lose what he has, doesn't have what he has) (182). One has to lose everything in order not to lose everything and, by ending on a note that exiles loss from this textual space, the loss of exile is rewritten more affirmatively as a rebirth of connexion through separation. But lodged tacitly within the text of *Manne* in very similar terms is the memory of Cixous's earlier explorations of how she herself came to writing in 'La Venue à l'écriture' ('Coming to Writing'): 'Et je dis: il faut avoir été aimée par la mort, pour naître et passer à l'écriture. La condition à laquelle commencer à écrire devient nécessaire – (et) – possible: *tout perdre*, avoir une fois tout perdu'[14] (And I say: you must have been loved by death to be born and move on to writing. The condition on which beginning to write becomes necessary – (and) – possible: *losing everything*, having once lost everything). Death launches the self into writing and is seen as a way of losing everything in order not to lose everything. In addition to this meditation on losing in order not to lose, 'La Venue' also contains the impossible motif of bearing witness to one's own death that recurs in *Manne* with reference to Mandelstam and Mandela. Significantly, the 'voile noire' that figures in the title of the subsequent related play, 'Voile noire, voile blanche', is also prefigured in this following passage from 'La Venue', pre-empting the connexion between *Manne* and 'Voile noire':

Besoin du Visage: de passer le mur, de déchirer la voile noire. De voir de mes yeux ce que je perds; de regarder la perte dans les yeux. Je veux voir de mes yeux la disparition. L'intolérable c'est que la mort n'ait pas lieu, qu'elle me soit dérobée. ('La Venue', 13)

(Need for the Face: to get past the wall, to tear up the black sail. To see my loss with my own eyes; to look loss in the eye. I want to see the disappearance with my own eyes. What's intolerable is that death might not take place, that I may be robbed of it.) ('Coming to Writing', 5)

This impossible act of witnessing death returns in *Manne*, and the questions, desires, and fears of Mandela and Mandelstam dovetail so well with their earlier counterpart in 'La Venue' that this intertextual polylogue actually speaks with one voice.

Entering into exile is figured for Mandela as entering into a living death. When Mandela's day of condemnation is recounted, the judgement is spoken about in terms of a deathless death; both he and the others who are convicted are described as being: 'Condamnés à mourir sans mort. Le présent arrêté, l'avenir rejeté au néant' (280) (Condemned to death without dying. The present arrested, the future cast back into nothingness) (206). This condemnation to a deathless death recalls the earlier description of Mandelstam's literal death without a witness: 'Malheureux les morts à qui l'on a volé non seulement leur vie mais aussi leur mort, car ils meurent à jamais sans arrêt' (25) (Unhappy the dead from whom we have stolen not only their life but also their death; they die forever without reprieve) (15). But these interminable deathless deaths are transformed into a desire to know the impossible in one of the textual visits to Mandelstam's poetry. Fear of death becomes a fervent desire to see beyond the end, 'de mourir sans mourir' (168) (to die without dying) (121). The impossible split that will enable the witness of death to testify to his own death leads to the assertion of a need for a companion: 'Il faut être deux pour mourir' (169) (One must be two to die) (121). The writing self of *Manne* provides the necessary companionship here, but only because she is already present – in a Cixousian echo from 'La Venue' – in the voicing of Mandelstam's and Mandela's desire for the impossible witness. While the 'je' of *Manne* appears to be as distant from the death of the other as the writing self of 'La Venue' is from the death she seeks to witness firsthand, she turns out finally to be at no great distance at all from the experience of the other. *Manne* instates the writing self as a responsible witness who acknowledges the impossibility of being able to step into the position of the other and to know their suffering and pain. Yet this impossibility is precisely what the text performs.

Without claiming their experiences explicitly as her own – since it is important that she remains on the side of life, on the side of the one who can live to tell the tale – the writing self bears witness to the deathless death of Mandela's exile and to Mandelstam's death without a witness. She crosses over to their side of the divide using a fluctuating narrative point of view, which gives her the appearance of not crossing over to their side fully and finally. The witness emerges through her own disappearance as the writing self fades so that the experiences of others may appear, but the self never disappears entirely: nothing is ever lost here. Such a preservation of self and other could be read as the most ethical of encounters, yet this encounter is enabled by the very factor that constitutes the ethical stumbling block in this text: the always already present 'je'. The accurate documentary facts from the lives of the Mandelas and the Mandelstams prevent this from being read solely as a text that tells us only about the writing self. But if we read this text in relation to its Cixousian intertext, we have a very different picture of the approach to these 'others' of *Manne*. This text does indeed bear witness to the impossible, but the impossible task here is that of allowing others to speak for themselves.

SARAH COOPER
University of Cambridge

NOTES

1 Hélène Cixous, *Manne aux Mandelstams aux Mandelas* (Paris, des femmes, 1988), p. 26; *Manna for the Mandelstams for the Mandelas*, translated by Catherine A. F. MacGillivray (Minneapolis, University of Minnesota Press, 1994), p. 15.
2 Maurice Blanchot, *Le Dernier à parler* (Paris, Fata Morgana, 1984), p. 9 (my translation).

3 See Morag Shiach, *Hélène Cixous: A Politics of Writing* (London, Routledge, 1991), pp. 101-5.
4 See Susan Sellers, *Hélène Cixous: Authorship, Autobiography and Love* (Cambridge, Polity Press, 1996). For a discussion of *Manne* that locates this text within a wider feminist project but which nonetheless focuses centrally on the issue of sexual difference, see also Martine Motard-Noar, '*Manne* ou Man: où en est l'écriture d'Hélène Cixous?', *The French Review* 66.2 (December 1992), 286-94.
5 Hélène Cixous, 'A propos de *Manne*', in *Hélène Cixous: Chemins d'une écriture*, edited by Françoise van Rossum-Guyon and Myriam Díaz-Diocaretz (Amsterdam, Rodopi, 1990), pp. 212-34 (p. 215).
6 Hélène Cixous, 'Voile noire, voile blanche/Black sail, White sail', translated by Catherine A. F. MacGillivray, *New Literary History* 25.2 (1994), 219-354.
7 Hélène Cixous, 'Le Rire de la Méduse', *L'Arc* 61 (1975), 39-54 (46); 'The Laugh of the Medusa', in *New French Feminisms: An Anthology*, edited by Elaine Marks and Isabelle de Courtivron (Amherst, University of Massachusetts Press, 1980), pp. 245-64 (p. 254).
8 See, for example, Sellers, *Hélène Cixous*, who explores how *Manne* uses Cixous's experiences of writing for the theatre 'to embody an alternative to the current order' (p. 94). See also, Verena Andermatt Conley, *Hélène Cixous* (Hemel Hempstead, Harvester Wheatsheaf, 1992), pp. 105-18, who links *Manne* to Cixous's plays that more directly address historical situations.
9 Hélène Cixous, 'De la scène de l'Inconscient à la scène de l'Histoire: Chemin d'une écriture', in Rossum-Guyon and Díaz-Diorcaretz, *Hélène Cixous: Chemins d'une écriture*, pp. 15-34 (p. 16); 'From the Scene of the Unconscious to the Scene of History', in *The Future of Literary Theory*, edited by Ralph Cohen (New York, Routledge, 1989), pp. 1-18 (p. 2).
10 Emmanuel Levinas, *Totalité et Infini: Essai sur l'extériorité* (The Hague, Livre de Poche, Martinus Nijhoff, 1971, first edition 1961), p. 26; *Totality and Infinity: An Essay on Exteriority*, translated by Alphonso Lingis (Pittsburgh, Duquesne University Press, 1969), p. 37.
11 Hélène Cixous, 'Difficult Joys', in *The Body and the Text: Hélène Cixous, Reading and Teaching*, edited by Helen Wilcox, Keith McWatters, Ann Thompson and Linda R. Williams (Hemel Hempstead, Harvester Wheatsheaf, 1990), pp. 5-30 (p. 12).
12 Julia Kristeva, 'Un nouveau type d'intellectuel: le dissident', *Tel Quel* 74 (Winter 1977), 3-8 (7); 'A New Type of Intellectual: The Dissident', in *The Kristeva Reader*, edited by Toril Moi (Oxford, Basil Blackwell, 1986), pp. 292-300 (p. 298).
13 Julia Kristeva, *Julia Kristeva: Interviews*, edited by Ross Mitchell Guberman (New York, Columbia University Press, 1996), p. 41.
14 Hélène Cixous, 'La Venue à l'écriture', in *Entre l'écriture* (Paris, des femmes, 1986), pp. 9-69 (p. 48); 'Coming to Writing', in *'Coming to Writing' and Other Essays*, edited by Deborah Jenson (Cambridge MA, Harvard University Press, 1991), pp. 1-58 (p. 38).

Millennial Fears: Fear, Hope and Transformation in Contemporary Feminist Writing

As the millennium comes to an end, and the twentieth century scarifies our fragile memory, very little will stand out in terms of epochal splendor.[1]

As Avital Ronell suggests, this is a cultural moment marked by the circulation of fear: a fear that is intimately connected to our memories, both individual and collective. The contemporary threatens our 'fragile memories' and disables us through fear. Fear, for Ronell, is bound up with our ethical appreciations of the meaning of risk: 'Ethical dilemmas of the present negotiate matters of life and death through indirect media and according to a question which has more to do with testing than with certainty. Whom do we expose to risk?' (xi). Risk involves the management of fear, but never its eradication. Ulrich Beck has written about risk as 'a systematic way of dealing with hazards and insecurities induced and introduced by modernization itself'.[2] 'Risk', for Beck, is the condition of the contemporary, but this risk is becoming increasingly abstract as it becomes increasingly prevalent in all aspects of social and individual life. Thus chemical, environmental or nuclear risks may be significant, but also invisible, and transgressive of boundaries of space and time: 'The focus is more and more on hazards which are neither visible nor perceptible to the victims; hazards that in some cases may not even take effect within the lifespans of those affected' (27). Reflecting on the 'often creeping, catastrophic potentials at the end of the twentieth century' (22), Beck suggests that our social and psychic structures may now be dominated by the ambiguous experience of risk. Risk may no longer be calculable or consistently manageable, it may in fact no longer be imaginable, and wealth is no necessary protector: 'parallel to the intensification of risk positions, the private escape routes and possibilities for compensation shrink and are simultaneously propagated' (36). For Beck, the contemporary intensification and abstraction of risk and the consequent circulation of anxiety have political consequences. He suggests a diminution of the utopian imagination in favour of a generalized defensiveness, 'basically, one is no longer concerned with attaining something "good", but rather with *preventing* the worst' (49).

Beck's analysis of the risk society and the potentially paralyzing effects of fear raises important questions about the possibilities of utopian imaginings and collective identities, 'How capable of compromise are anxiety-producing communities of danger? In what forms of action will they organize?' (49). The aim of this article is to consider the implications of the intensification of fear and the circulation of anxieties for the cultural and political project that is contemporary feminism. In particular, I will be considering the importance of fear in recent texts by Judith Butler, Seyla Benhabib, Sadie Plant, and Hélène Cixous. Reading Cixous's recent writings within this broader cultural movement may, of course, be seen as either surprising or provocative, since 'feminism' is a space with which she has never comfortably identified. The motifs and images that resonate between the texts I will examine may in themselves provide some sort of justification for the reading I propose, but my claim in reading Cixous within the cultural parameters of contemporary feminism is in fact rather stronger. In the disruptions and the complexities of her texts I find a crucial though perturbing space for the understanding of the lived experience of sexual difference, as well as a fragile but persistent utopian imagination. And it is the possibility of a utopian moment, the collective and individual construction of hope, that is so contested by the intensification of our millennial fears.

Judith Butler's *Excitable Speech: A Politics of the Performative* was published in 1997. In some ways, this book is a development of Butler's work in *Gender Trouble*, which had explored the ways in which 'gender' is a performative category rather than a substantive or fixed identity.[3] *Excitable Speech* returns to the questions of resistance and transgression implicit in that earlier text, this time in relation to the political and legal understandings of 'hate speech'. In American legal discourse 'excitable speech' refers to statements given by individuals who are in some sense coerced, who are not in control of their own speech, but for Butler, 'excitable speech' becomes a compelling metaphor for the complex relations between language, identity, and agency. Butler's theoretical framework is derived from an Althusserian analysis of subjectivity and a Foucauldian theorization of power. Thus subjectivity, and gender, are produced by systems of representation. Butler considers the relations between language, violence, and fear: 'Why do the names that the subject is called appear to instill the fear of death and the question of whether or not one will survive? Why should a merely linguistic address produce such a response of fear?'[4] For Butler, we are all vulnerable to language because we are all linguistic beings: we exist as subjects through processes of interpellation. We come to recognize ourselves, to be our selves, through moments of recognition where we respond to a series of namings: 'The terms that facilitate recognition are themselves conventional, the effects and instruments of a social ritual that decides, often through exclusion and violence, the linguistic conditions of survivable subjects' (5). Throughout *Excitable Speech* the subject is understood to be under threat from and within language. As a bodily and a gendered being, Butler argues, one is continually under threat from the very linguistic system within which one must live and negotiate one's identity. Language bears the marks of social exclusions and thus to inhabit a linguistic system is to live in a state of fear. Something of this power of language to exclude and to disable is registered by Cixous in a recent text which deals with her memories of childhood in Algeria. She remembers hearing the phrase 'don't be a jew', and wondering what it could mean while 'for the other girls that expression was a normal part of French culture'.[5]

For Butler, our linguistic being is both disabling and enabling. In the temporal and intersubjective nature of language Butler finds, in one sense, the source of its power to wound. Speech always resonates with past speech and speeches to come, and any given speech act inhabits a temporality that must always escape the individual subject, 'an "act" is not a momentary happening, but a certain nexus of temporal horizons, the condensation of an iterability that exceeds the moment it occasions' (14). If language were not intersubjective, if it did not contain a sedimentation of the past and an opening towards the future, there would be no possibility of recognizing ourselves as individual subjects, 'the time of discourse, even in its radical incommensurability with the time of the subject *makes possible* the speaking time of the subject' (28). As a social and historical system, then, language bears the marks of systems of power, it carries the traces of various forms of barbarism. But its temporality also, for Butler, signals its incompleteness. If language is fundamentally enmeshed in history then it is also always in flux, and can then open out to spaces that are new, disturbing, or oppositional. Butler is cautious about the limits of such a model of resistance within language, and admits it to be a fragmentary and fragile model of agency, but insists that it is at least imaginable:

The name one is called both subordinates and enables, producing a sense of agency from ambivalence, a set of effects that exceed the animating intentions of the call. (…) Insurrectionary speech becomes the necessary response to injurious language, a risk taken in response to being put at risk, a repetition in language that forces change. (163)

So 'insurrectionary speech' becomes a matter of risk, perhaps in Beck's sense of risk as a way of managing the hazards and insecurities of the contemporary. It puts the self in danger, continually oscillating between fear and hope. Such insurrectionary speech becomes, for Butler, the possibility of acting politically through 'opening new contexts, speaking in ways that have never yet been legitimated' (41).

We can find the same search for new modes of thought in the work of Seyla Benhabib, who situates her philosophical and political project in opposition to what she understands by 'the postmodern'. Benhabib sees the tensions between feminism and postmodernism as both a displacement and a development of the question that 'haunted' feminist theory a decade earlier: 'the uneasy relations of marxism and feminism'.[6] At stake is the possibility of a philosophical knowledge that might be more than contingent, since Benhabib argues that 'social criticism without philosophy is not possible' (25). She seeks to sustain the viability of autonomy as a political and philosophical goal, and to ground the notion of the metaphysical in relation to the political and ethical concerns of feminism. Benhabib's commitment is to 'a regulative principle of hope' without which 'not only morality but also radical transformation is unthinkable', and she articulates the desire for a form of thinking that reaches out to the 'wholly other', and strives towards that which is not yet (30). But the 'practical-moral imperative' towards such new forms of thought is, like feminist theory itself, haunted, in this case by the force of the philosophical positions Benhabib disavows. She speaks of haunting, of a troubled alliance, of the end of a project, of a political retreat, and her dramatization of the possible collapse of the philosophical project as she understands it is both vivid and marked by fear:

Once we have detranscendentalized, contextualized, historicized, genderized the subject of knowledge, the context of inquiry, and even the methods of justification, what remains of philosophy? Does not philosophy become a form of genealogical critique of regimes of discourse and power as they succeed each other in their endless historical monotony? Or maybe philosophy becomes a form of thick cultural narration of the sort that hitherto only poets have provided us with? (25)

The voices of poets resonate also within Cixous's recent *Messie*, where they do not signify the negation of philosophy but rather a textual space beyond the philosophical. The characters in this fiction set off on a journey, a journey that will go along roads and through towns where we will encounter fears, memories, various animals and magical beings, and also from time to time glimpse the possibility of hope. Every moment within this text is lived and narrated with a striking intensity:

> Quelle vie que leur vie si longue elle vaut bien neuf vies mais si longue soit-elle en apparence, si l'on peut appeler longue une vie, cette vie n'a aucune longueur; on dirait une foudre successive. Sans quotidien. Comme s'il n'y avait qu'un seul jour sans coupure un seul souffle sans usure. Sans tranquillité. Des fragments du temps général, en fusion dans leur creuset.[7]

> (What a life their life that is so long it is worth nine lives but though it appears long, if one can call a life long, this life has no length: it is more a series of flashes of lightning. Without the everyday. As if there were only one single day without breaks one single breath without exhaustion. Without tranquillity. Fragments of time in general, in fusion within their crucible.)

This 'series of flashes of lightning' risks overwhelming any sense of temporal continuity within the text, as the image of fusion suggests. The intensity and the lack of the everyday both tend towards the fragmentation of identities. The month of August seems to be the moment of greatest risk for the characters in *Messie*: 'C'était toujours au mois d'août, le coup, l'adieu, tous deux redoutaient août et ses envoûtements. En août on pouvait mourir ou devenir fou…' (31) (It was always in the month of August, the blow, the farewell, both dreaded August and its bewitchment. In August one could die, or go mad). The month of August is dominated by fear, which is repeatedly invoked in the section of the text entitled 'States of August':

> En août tout était à craindre ils se craignaient, il craignait tout d'elle, qu'elle fût bonne, qu'elle fût mauvaise, qu'elle fût forte qu'elle fût malade, qu'elle fût présente, qu'elle fût absente, qu'elle fût sienne, qu'elle fût lui, qu'elle fût autre. (31)

> (In August everything had to be feared they feared each other, he feared everything that came from her, her being good, her being bad, her being strong her being ill, her presence, her absence, her being his, her being him, her being other.)

The month of August is haunted by past events, by the turbulence of memories and desires, and by griefs so intense that they threaten to overwhelm. The two characters within this fragment of the text are crippled by fear: the winds of August paralyze them both. The man struggles to construct some sense of connectedness, but finds himself 'étourdi, tremblant, le poil hérissé, la peau du visage étirée par les peurs' (32) (Dazed, trembling, hair standing on end, the skin of his face taut with fear). This fear is intimately connected to the experience of passion:

Nous ne pouvons pas être sans tomber, nous ne pouvons pas être noués d'amour sans tombe ouverte sans cordes sans clous sans perforation sans pneumothorax sans pertes de jambes sans crainte pour souffle et inhalation de vent embrasé pour boisson. (34)

(We cannot be without falling, we cannot be wrapped up in love without an open tomb without ropes without nails without perforation without pneumothorax without loss of legs without fear for breath and burning wind for liquid sustenance.)

This mutual implication of fear and passion is particularly striking in Cixous's most recent fiction, *Osnabrück*. This text explores the desires and fears that circulate round and within the figure of the mother, a mother, like Cixous's own mother, who is called Eve. The early sections of the novel resonate with the narrator's fears as she reconstructs scenes of abandonment, isolation and loss. The Prologue begins, 'A l'âge de trois ans et demi je perdis ma mère'[8] (At the age of three and a half I lost my mother). She is standing outside her school, overwhelmed by grief, unable to move, incapable of entering the school and of willing the separation from her mother. This moment of crisis brings the narrator towards nothingness, thrusts her outside time: 'J'étais impossible. Je n'étais plus moi. J'étais énorme et rien, je me passai toute en dehors du temps' (10) (I was impossible. I was no longer me. I was vast and I was nothing, I happened apart from time). This episode prefigures many of the moments of loss and fear that will emerge in *Osnabrück*, and like these episodes carries the weight of both psychic and political histories. The school which is the scene of this crisis of loss and negation is a temporary jewish school set up to cater for the children who have been excluded from other schools because of the anti-jewish laws enacted by the Vichy government. So the narrator's loss can be read not simply through the narrative of maternal separation but also through the exclusions and violences of that political history.

When the narrator finally manages to enter the school, with the help of her brother, she also enters the world of writing. She is, she says, still vulnerable to griefs and to passions that exceed her, but in writing there is a moment of jubilation. Writing becomes, quite literally at the level of the signifier, her mother: 'avec mes mamans de papier. Première drogue' (12) (with my mothers of paper. The first drug). This identification with textuality, and its relation to the experience of maternal loss, becomes increasingly enmeshed in the writing of death:

Je pense à mourir. Cette nuit, j'ai rêvé que j'avais la tuberculose. (...) Elle est à la porte, la mort, me disant : je suis là, moi la fin. Et moi incrédule disant, mais je suis trop jeune, que va dire mon amant? Et maman ne me croira pas. (...) Souvent j'ai peur qu'elle meure avant moi, c'est logique. Mais pas toujours. (...) Parfois j'ai peur qu'elle meure. C'est la peur même cette peur. C'est ce que je ne peux pas écrire, cette mort de l'écriture. (31-2)

(I am thinking about dying. Last night I dreamt that I had tuberculosis. (...) It is at my door, death, saying to me: I am here, I, the end. And I am incredulous and saying, but I am too young, what will my lover say? And my mother will not believe me. (...) Often I am afraid that she will die before me, it's logical. But not always. (...) Sometimes I am afraid that it will die. This fear is fear itself. It's what I cannot write, this death of writing.)

The narrator's fears of separation and of death and her identification with writing are initially set against the rationality and pragmatism of her mother. The mother is committed to the power and reality of the lived moment which provides a defence against crippling fear, 'Eve Cixous, la sage-femme qui ne craint rien' (103) (Eve Cixous, the midwife who fears nothing). But this dichotomy between the writing self and the pragmatic self is increasingly undermined as the text dramatizes Eve's struggle within and against time. Eve's own history is marked by loss and by separations which carry within them the conflicts of recent political history. Her husband is lost, at first metaphorically through his designation as 'your father' rather than 'my husband', and then by his cruelly early death. Eve's practical relation to both life and death is increasingly undermined by her struggle to attribute responsibility and agency in the matter of dying. Her husband, she tells her daughter, would still be alive if he had not exhausted himself by returning to general practice and she reprimands her daughter for working too hard and putting herself at risk of death: 'Quand je te vois je vois Tonpère tu crois que ça me fait plaisir j'ai toujours peur qu'il ne reste plus rien que du papier dit ma mère' (193) (When I see you I see Yourfather you think that gives me pleasure I am always terrified that there will be nothing left but paper says my mother).

The struggle with time and with writing, and the attempt to narrate death, continue to the end of *Osnabrück* which oscillates between passion and separation, between hope and fear. The compulsive doubling of mother and daughter is inflected by the compelling presence of the narrator's brother, who narrates both his murderous feelings towards his mother in the past and his very belated struggle towards autonomy. Mother and daughter set off on a trip to the cemetery, which may represent some attempt to share in each other's fears about and fantasies of death, but they never arrive. The fiction nearly ends with a passionate plea for closeness, 'la passion de maman, une minute d'amour, je donnerais le livre pour la tenir encore une minute dans mes bras et me réchauffer l'âme à la chaleur de ma maman' (228) (the passion of my mother, a minute of love, I would give this book to hold her for one minute more in my arms and to warm my soul with the warmth of my mother). But at the last minute a trip to Osnabrück is proposed. It is time to confront the weight of the past, but, at least in this fiction, they never arrive at their journey's end. Instead the fiction ends with two brief images that bring us back to its beginning. The narrator declares this book impossible to write, and then evokes a poignant moment of domestic intimacy, where 'Eve épluche les oignons et je verse un torrent de larmes' (230) (Eve peels the onions and I shed a flood of tears).

Much of Cixous's recent writing explores the haunting of the self in the present by the traumas and losses of a much larger history. Registering the legacy of these larger histories is already implicit in Cixous's theatrical work, or in her commitment to a series of writers who have been persecuted and dispossessed. But in her recent fiction the experience of oppression has become more fully part of the inner struggle and the unconscious of her characters, and the fears that circulate in these texts have become somehow more insistent. Cixous has indeed written about her relation to fear in 'Love of the Wolf', an essay published in *Stigmata, Escaping Texts* in 1998.[9] She begins by invoking Clarice Lispector's account of the relations between trauma and fear, and then goes on to explore the psychic fascination with fear that lies behind erotic relationships: 'There is no love except where there is fear. Love run by fear, escorted by fear' (89). This fear is generated partly by the cruelty and violence that are within all intense intersubjective relationships, but is also connected to the recognition of death that is triggered by the experience of the erotic: 'as soon as I love, death is there, it camps out right in the middle of my body, in daylight, getting mixed up with my food, dispatching from the far-off future its prophetic presence, taking the bread out of my mouth' (86).

In 'The Love of the Wolf' we find an exploration of the pleasures of being terrified, a reprise of the childhood game of hide and seek: 'How good it feels to be lost, to be looked for, to be found, to tremble with all these fears together' (90). This is a markedly more celebratory account of fear than is found in either *Osnabrück* or *Messie*, perhaps because the 'trauma' that lies behind such fear is metaphorized as the fairy-tale wolf, a less terrifying figure than the figures of history who haunt so much of her recent fiction. The characters in *Messie* know the experience of a love marked by fear and pain, but they also try to imagine and to construct moments of hope, even if such hope can only ever be fleeting: 'Ne sommes-nous pas les descendants de petites tragédies qui sont arrivées à nos ancêtres les chèvres et les chevaux à huit pattes! Ancêtres par alliance de peines et d'espérances' (*Messie*, 19) (Are we not the descendants of little tragedies which befell our ancestors the goats and the horses with eight hooves! Ancestors by marriage of sufferings and hopes). In the dramatic episodes and the imagery of *Messie* there is a movement between fear and hope, even while there is a passionate commitment to the transformative potential of fear itself. The female character insists that she does not want an end to conflict, but only a truce: 'Sainte Crainte ma soeur fiancée de l'espoir frissons de mes joies, aile gauche de mon ange gardien, ne m'abandonne jamais' (46) (Holy Fear my sister betrothed to hope shuddering with my joys, left wing of my guardian angel, never abandon me). Fear is betrothed to hope, but in this text its appearance is always something of a surprise: 'C'était l'étonnement. Le rire qui avait secoué l'arche de Noé lorsque l'étrave avait rudement frappé l'Ararat parce que dans la cale en vérité plus personne n'y croyait, et malgré tout on espérait' (46) (It was astonishment. The laughter which shook Noah's Ark when the keel collided harshly with Mount Ararat because inside the hold, in truth, no-one believed in it, but despite everything they hoped).

During the truce, which is a concrete moment within the text, there are indeed moments when nobody fears anything. There is a practical experiment in hope, or perhaps in refusing fear. After the entry of the cat into the text, it becomes possible to imagine each other differently, and to think of a world without fear:

> 'elle cède à un chat,
> elle perd la raison,' (...)
> elle abjurait la peur et l'ignorance et elle se promettait de ne pas renier l'innocent mystère animal et de le respecter dans son chat. (65)
>
> ('she gives way to a cat,
> she loses her reason,' (...)
> she forswore fear and ignorance and she promised herself not to deny the innocent and animal mystery and to respect it in her cat.)

This renunciation of fear, though evasive, is continually desired throughout *Messie*. Later, in the fragment that leads us 'from the menagerie to philosophy' we are told that 'c'est urgent. L'impératif d'espoir'

(103) (it is urgent. The imperative for hope), and we can read *Messie* partly as an exploration of different possible responses to this imperative.

The tools necessary to construct a philosophy and a practice of hope are derived from a wide range of literary and philosophical texts. The female character talks about the slowness and the recalcitrance of her attempts to think beyond the paralysis of fear:

Personne ne peut imaginer la lenteur de mon char de pensée, nous roulons à quelques centimètres par mois et peut-être par an, ce n'est pas l'immobilité absolue mais toute la douleur monstrueuse du déplacement paralysé. (109)

(No-one can imagine the slowness of my thinking waggon, we travel at a few centimetres per month perhaps even per year, it is not absolute immobility but all the monstrous suffering of a static displacement.)

In this part of the text, she is struggling to think about what might be the essence of poetry, though she never manages to arrive at any such essence. She feels threatened by the voices around her which are demanding a categorical answer to this problem, and she offers instead images that might suggest some of the contours of a possible answer, such as 'la Poésie est un hérisson' (111) (Poetry is a hedgehog). She does not want to see too clearly, but rather values her short-sightedness as a means of perceiving differently.

Epic literature provides one of the spaces in which the characters, and the readers, of *Messie* can glimpse the contours of another mode of thought: the space of the castle. The woman decides to treat her short-sightedness so that she can perceive more clearly this site which is so central to a whole tradition of poetic writing. The castle condenses and embodies a history of poetic representation and a legacy of recalcitrant hope:

Il y en a un, dans tous les poèmes épiques eddique homérique biblique babylonien, pour commencer, dès qu'un monde commence, arrive le Château, le désir du Château, d'être construit détruit désiré tenté, de tenter de l'édifier en un seul hiver et pas plus de trois, avec l'aide d'un cheval magique ou sinon d'une chèvre. (120)

(There is one in all epics, the eddas, Homer, bible stories, Gilgamesh, to begin with, as soon as a world begins, the castle enters, the desire of the castle, to be built, destroyed, desired, attempted, to try to build it in a single winter and no more than three, with the help of a magic horse or else of a goat.)

One might even imagine the possibility here of reading the whole of *Messie*, with its quests, its supernatural transformations, its battles, and its magical beasts, as a sort of epic poem which dramatizes the struggle between hope and fear.

But poetry in itself cannot sustain the desired absence of fear. The necessity of intersubjective relations, so heavy a burden throughout most of the text, becomes, at moments, also a site of hope. The woman and the man fail to meet while they are on a journey to Pompeii: they are doomed to inhabit two distinct logical universes which drive them apart, and they lose each other. But finally they do find themselves together, and the fraught and anxious experiences of separation and loss give way to a moment of utopian imagining: 'Et maintenant ils avaient manqué le bateau, leur excursion s'arrêtait au port, mais enfin ils étaient ensemble. Assis sur le banc ils pensent au livre de leur sort et ils espèrent' (130-1) (And now they had missed the boat, their excursion was ending at the port, but at last they were together. Sitting on the bench they thought about the book of their fate and they hoped).

The woman learns, at the end of the fiction, to be wary of the urge for clarity and to seek out ambiguity. In the experience of erotic love she finds a kind of negation of the will to know. Like the passion between Tristan and Isolde, the life of this woman is marked by a series of disruptions and shocks. The telephone becomes a metaphorical figure for the compelling experience of intersubjectivity, and for the effects of the networks of texts and subjectivities through which one is obliged to live the contemporary: 'impossible de les imaginer sans le téléphone. Pour corriger leur myopie de vie il y avait l'ange bizarre avec sa tête de cadran et les petites ailes raides' (147) (impossible to imagine them without the telephone. In order to correct their short-sightedness in relation to life there was the bizarre angel with a face like a dial and little rigid wings). '*N'aie pas peur*' (152) (*don't be afraid*), *Messie* tells us, but by the end of the fiction the castle is destroyed, chronological time is restored, and eternity can no longer even be glimpsed.

A related textual and philosophical struggle between fear and hope within the contemporary can also be discerned in Sadie Plant's *Zeros + Ones: Digital Women + the New Technoculture*. This book draws on a number of genres to develop its cultural history and its philosophical speculations, including the novelistic. It is concerned with technology, and particularly with cyberculture, and explores the meanings and implications of technological change for the experience of the everyday, and particularly for the everyday life of women. Plant places herself within the space of cyberfeminism, in the sense that she sees within the social and cultural transformations bound up with technological innovations real possibilities of resistance or of liberation for women. Drawing on the modes of communication and of interaction rendered possible by new forms of technology, Plant wants to imagine new and disturbing forms of subjectivity. She is interested in the new kinds of identity that might be constructed and imagined through the physical and virtual spaces that become possible only through technological change. Her aim in *Zeros + Ones* is to discern and to propagate innovative modes of thought, and patterns of living that will be creative and transgressive.

The structure of her text is fragmentary. She draws on a diverse series of texts, weaving together a series of anecdotes and allusions, and offers us a sort of textual collage of questions, histories, stories, and images. She consciously looks for a textual equivalent of the open-endedness and complex intertextuality of contemporary computer cultures. She also aims to provide metaphors and narratives for thinking about technology that will disturb the apparently inevitable masculinization of that technology. Thus there are fragments dedicated to 'genderquake', to 'casting on' and 'casting off', to 'speed queens', to 'hysteresis' and to 'cyberflesh', all of which tend to remove technology from the realm of the sublime while placing it back within the productive and unpredictable space of the social. If there is one organizing narrative within *Zeros + Ones*, however, it is the narrative of the life and the writings of Ada Lovelace, the inventor of the Analytical Engine which embodied the first example of what would later be called computer programming:

Ada Augusta King, Countess of Lovelace; Ada Lovelace née Byron; A.A.L., the first programmer. She is also Ada, the language of the United States military machine. 'She is the Queen of Engines, the Enchantress of Number'.[10]

Ada is in some sense the heroine of *Zeros + Ones*, but she is also its enigma. She is the hysteric who was ill for most of her life and had frequent attacks of fainting and of paralysis, and she is a victim but she is also the creative and transgressive impulse that is so important to Plant's overall argument. She is the figure of hope. Ada Lovelace was Byron's daughter, and she was also a friend of the mathematicians Charles Babbage and Mary Somerville and an unusually talented mathematician herself. Crippled by illness all her life, and dying in 1852 at the age of only thirty-six, she nonetheless left a body of mathematical work of exceptional originality. She did not want to think or to speculate in terms of received categories, but rather, 'Ada was hunting for something that would do more than represent an existing world. Something that would work: something new, something else' (31). She also enjoyed a career as a passionate gambler, leaving at the time of her death very substantial debts.

Ada is a woman ahead of her time, an invalid, an errant and capricious woman, but also the mathematician who made possible the age of cyberculture. In her life and writings Plant finds the ambiguities that circulate through any attempt to think the social and psychic meanings of our millennial culture. One of the texts Plant draws on in her exploration of Ada Lovelace is *The Difference Engine* by William Gibson and Bruce Sterling, and it is with a reading of a passage from that text, which is woven into the overall fabric of *Zeros + Ones*, that I will conclude this article:

> The passions suffer no less by this gaming fever than the understanding and the imagination. What vivid, unnatural hope and fear, joy and anger, sorrow and discontent burst out all at once upon a roll of the dice, a turn of the card...! Who can consider without indignation that all those womanly affections, which should have been consecrated to children and husband, are thus vilely prostituted and thrown away. I cannot but be grieved when I see the Gambling Lady fretting and bleeding inwardly from such evil and unworthy obsessions; when I behold the face of an angel agitated by the heart of a fury.[11]

Within this passage, as within Plant's text as a whole, I find echoes of the millennial fears articulated across the range of texts I have explored within this article, but also traces of the struggle to think and to imagine differently. Ada is associated with both hope and fear, though these are both described as unnatural. All of Ada's feelings are stigmatized under the space of 'the unnatural', and even her maternal emotions are prostituted. Her body is marked and bleeding inwardly under the weight of her transgressive obsessions. She lives in a world of absolute chance, where her whole self is perpetually at risk. She lives with and through risk because she does not know how to live differently: here again, perhaps, she is ahead of her time. In the end, this is her destiny: she is forced to live with risk because stasis is so unthinkable for her. Like the characters in *Messie*, this woman is riven between the angel and the fury. And the heart of the fury might remind us also of Cixous's *La Ville parjure ou le réveil des Erinyes*, a play in which the force of the Furies is unleashed to embody very contemporary fears. The angel and the fury battle within Plant's text for the body and the soul of this woman who carries within her so much of the future. Plant's version of the contemporary is marked by violence, by risk, and by the passions of this Gambling Lady who, despite her death, returns to the surface of this text to talk to us, hesitantly and intermittently, about hope.

MORAG SHIACH
Queen Mary and Westfield College,
University of London

NOTES

1 Avital Ronell, *Finitude's Score: Essays for the End of the Millennium* (Lincoln, Nebraska, University of Nebraska Press, 1994), p. ix.
2 Ulrich Beck, *Risk Society: Towards a New Modernity*, translated by Mark Ritter (London, Sage, 1992), p. 21.
3 Judith Butler, *Gender Trouble: Feminism and the Subversion of Identity* (London, Routledge, 1990).
4 Judith Butler, *Excitable Speech: A Politics of the Performative* (London, Routledge, 1997), p. 5.
5 Hélène Cixous, 'Letter to Zohra Drif', *Parallax* 4:2 (1998), 189-196 (191).
6 Seyla Benhabib, 'Feminism and Postmodernism: An Uneasy Alliance', in Seyla Benhabib, Judith Butler, Drucilla Cornell and Nancy Fraser, *Feminist Contentions: A Philosophical Exchange* (London, Routledge, 1995), pp. 17-34 (p. 17).
7 Hélène Cixous, *Messie* (Paris, des femmes, 1996), pp. 15-16.
8 Hélène Cixous, *Osnabrück* (Paris, des femmes, 1999), p. 9.
9 Hélène Cixous, 'Love of the Wolf', translated by Keith Cohen, in *Stigmata, Escaping Texts* (London, Routledge, 1998), pp. 84-99.
10 Sadie Plant, *Zeros + Ones: Digital Women + the New Technoculture* (London, Fourth Estate, 1997), p. 27.
11 William Gibson and Bruce Sterling, *The Difference Engine* (London, VGSF, 1991), p. 366, cited in Plant, p. 29.

An Interview with Hélène Cixous[1]

Ian Blyth: Since we are conducting this interview in English, it seems appropriate to start with your multicultural background and with what you call your 'foreign relationship to the French language'.[2] I'd like to ask you how you feel about your books, which are originally written in French, being translated into other languages; and, following on from that, how does this affect your use of neologisms?

Hélène Cixous: There are several questions here, so let me separate them a little – although you are right, they belong to a general issue. First of all, I think – and this is of course my own vision of writing, my own *parti pris* in writing – that to write is to make a language foreign. I don't even like to say to *make*, rather to *foreign* the language. I can't imagine that I write French, or that I am a French writer: usually I refer to my practice in language as not French, but Free-ench. Either you reproduce, either you remain within the boundaries of a received and so-called correct socialized language (I mean writing, and again I have to make a distinction between what I call writing, or *écriture*, or text, and literature; of course everything I do I inscribe within the field or concept of literature, but I think that it's misleading, because we call 'literature' everything that is published…), whereas what I do, the only exercise inside or through language which I think is worth the pain and joy, is, on the contrary, to revolutionize language as it is used. I have always felt that I belonged to the tribe of those who turmoil language. Otherwise I'm not interested. I mean, I could just read a newspaper.

French is multilingual, it has been grafted diversely and is composed largely of Latin etc., but then it has been invaded, it has appropriated so many signifiers coming from all kinds of languages, which, of course ordinary French people do not know about. It is exactly like a country: it pretends to be pure but it is impure. But then French itself, or *herself* – in French, as you know, *la langue* is feminine – can also be open to political distortions, or to the exploitation of all the subtleties of its rhetoric: it can produce/generate all kinds of unexpected effects. It's the unexpectedness of the language which I am interested in. The play of genres, genders, homonyms, the aptitude to ambiguity, amphibology, a general resource of indecisiveness.

I.B.: Do you think this comes across in translation?

H.C.: It's what makes it untranslatable. It's the main problem. Of course, this is the case for all writers who write in this way, it's the case of Joyce and all so-called experimental writers. All writers who are adventurous in language are untranslatable. So: how to translate them? It requires a person who knows about the issues and who has an ear for languages. And, since you cannot save or preserve the special effects in language (I mean the signifiers), you cannot find equivalence in the arrival language, you have to look for equivalence by displacing the effects. I know a little about what happens in English translations because I can check, because I can work with translators and make suggestions. But I know that it's extremely difficult. The translator has to be faithful by being unfaithful, by being in a very subtle and calculated way unfaithful in order to be faithful. On one of my recent books, for instance, which is called *Or, les lettres de mon père*, I have been working with an Italian translator, a scholar, who has done her dissertation with me, and it's great. I don't know Italian, but we discussed it all the time. She would come to me with a page where she had met with a number of 'impossibilities': she couldn't save *this* play on signifiers so she was looking for some way in which what was lost could be recaptured a little later by a choice of signifiers in Italian. We would check together as to whether it came to an equivalent result in meaning and in sound. For me it was a delicate challenge, I enjoyed it; and she would tell me that it wakened *her* to the treasures hidden in Italian: she realized that she had to make her use of Italian freer and more inventive. But then of course that's the ideal situation, when I can discuss things in sympathy with a translator. Not that I want to impose anything, but it's very difficult for a translator to take the risk and the responsibility, to give up something here and, on the contrary, invent something there.

I imagine (though I have never checked) that in all my books there are probably about a hundred neologisms – that is, words that I make up and which are completely 'readable' in French. The French reader is not surprised if, for instance, I use the word *oublire*, which all my translators have had to negotiate with. *Oublire* is a kind of portmanteau word composed of *oublier*, to forget, and *lire*, to read: through this invention I indicated that you cannot read without forgetting: it's the same paradoxical mechanism that is at work. Reading erased in order to open to rereading etc. The French reader of course notices that *oublire* does not exist, yet can guess the necessity of it: indeed it works in French, in the music of French, but you cannot render *oublire* in other languages. You cannot render it as harmoniously in English, or in German, or in Italian, so they all had to look for equivalents.

I.B.: You seem drawn to the idea of the impossible, of 'thinking the unthinkable'.[3] One sees this very clearly in the reference to 'Hokusai's truth' in *FirstDays of the Year*, where 'it is only the impossibility of ever painting Fujiyama [that authorizes] the painter to paint and attempt to paint his entire life'.[4] Do you see your writing as operating within this *différance*, this always searching, never arriving? It's always in the middle: it aims for somewhere it knows it will never reach and that is what gives it its *raison d'être*?

H.C.: Yes, in a way, although I don't think I'd formulate it in terms of a *raison d'être*. This is not something I decided beforehand, or that I had a theory about, but gradually I realized that I was always in the same race: I was pursuing or hunting something that escapes and, if I didn't want to be dishonest, I had to follow the movement of the thinking, of the story. Eventually there is no end: the book closes and the quest goes on. Looking backwards I realized that this was constitutive of everything *I* do, but also of everything that I think most artists are prone to experiencing. That is, making every effort to reach not a visible aim, but something secret, which has an appeal. Of course what is important is that link between secret and appeal, the fact that we are yearning for or called by the existence of something that escapes. It seems paradoxical, because you do not know what it is, but you perceive/sense signs… Which is why I can use the metaphors of painting. You see that what the painter is running after is light, the secret of light, the root of light, which of course is multiform and impossible to catch. I feel how for the painter it must be excruciating to paint a painting because a picture is doomed to the frame, whereas what a painter as poet is trying to paint is movement and what disappears. Painters have to capture the essence, they have to conjure up what disappears. It is exactly the same in writing. What I do is just to deal with what is appearing and disappearing *in the same moment*. Of course, when I speak in those terms it seems abstract, but in my books it is concrete, it is a concrete situation. It refers to an event, or a person, or a character that/who embodies this structure of appearance-disappearance, or to some theme or fact that has to be told and which resists the telling. So actually what is being written is the saga of all the efforts to conquer what you will never conquer. Virginia Woolf's *The Waves* is that: it is just circling around something, around somebody: not reaching it. It doesn't mean of course that this is negative…

I.B.: I suppose caught up within this, is the idea of writing in the present: grabbing things 'in the instant they pass', because if you do not grab them, they will be 'lost forever'.[5] Is this why you always have a notebook with you?

H.C.: Well I don't *always*. For instance, here, I don't have it. I don't even know whether I've brought it. Although, I've used it: well maybe I do have it [*laughs*], but you know there must be circumstances, there must be places where I *can't* do that. But the moment a something flashes – which can be of course an anything; it's always unexpected – I try to note *it* down because I know that five minutes later its itness will have vanished totally, even from my memory. It's not because I am a miser, it's simply because this is absolutely exceptional: it's something that has been given, which is irreplaceable and if I don't make the effort to note it down immediately it's as if it never had happened. So, in a way I feel that I have to be – for myself, for my enjoyment – the keeper of what goes by in such a transitory way. I guess artists and writers all do that: they will jot down. Twenty years ago, for instance, I came upon the similar traces and fragments that Clarice Lispector had scribbled on a chequebook. I would do that – i.e. write on a cheque – it's an indication that what is important is that when I speak to you and I'm completely with you, I also see the movement, which is extremely soft and delicate, of the end of a branch with foliage which simply swerves there and is very beautiful. And of course, this instant is *that*: it's inside and outside and that very slight movement which corresponds to what we are doing. If I am not aware of all those details, there's no writing.

I.B.: So this is where your books come from?

H.C.: That's the climate of the book, but my books are actually philosophical in essence; they come from analysable events. There is a big event, whatever it is, and I never invent it: it *has* to happen, you cannot invent great events [*laughs*]. Which is something that I have learned. When I was a kid I figured out that you could invent everything, but that's not true: you don't invent, you only discover. What I perceive, or what I receive is the mystery, it's something that is totally mysterious, but that has deep roots that are related to human fate and what makes for life and death etc. – by which I mean all the great issues of human destiny: passion, or mourning, or treason, or brutal disappointment etc. So what I deal with is always something that has to do with drama, it's the drama of a certain passion. But then, of course, it becomes embodied in the concreteness of life, which is made of flesh, branches, animals... and babies [*laughs*].

I.B.: Finally, could I ask you about the idea of horses in your work. You have talked of the horses in Kleist and Clarice Lispector in terms of a 'gallop[ing] freely',⁶ and of writing as being 'carried away on the backs of these funny horses that are metaphors'.⁷ And then, there is the question running through *Promethea*: is she a woman, is she a horse? Is there any special reason behind this?

H.C.: [*laughs*] Actually, no, but it is a good remark, because this is part of my unconscious. I suppose that horses are metaphorical animals: they themselves are metaphors; I have never had a horse and I have almost never touched a horse: they belong to a kind of mythical reign. Maybe it's because the rhythm of a horse is very inspiring – the gallop, as you picked it up. Probably what is obvious to anybody is the decomposition of the movement: the fact that they run on four legs, differently: the four legs have a different state of rest and a different activity. At the same time the process gathers together a huge momentum which, for me, relates to what writing does: it's a gathering of different forces that are harmonious... but of course I am trying to rationalize: I didn't when I picked up the horse. What I think is most important is the fact that it is a metaphor. A long time ago I recognized, as if it were in one of my dreams, the presence of the horse in a fragment by Kafka called 'The Wish to Be a Red Indian'. It has two or three lines, with only the mane. I mean the horse doesn't exist: there is only the mane like a faery fan, you're just gripping the mane and it's just like that branch – it's the ends, the most refined extremity of movement, it's the allusion and at the same time it's the illusion of the body. But then, there's something else. It's the fact that animals are important for me because I can't imagine human beings other than as animals in transition. They *are* animals for me and, if they're not, they're not interesting. I need the instinctiveness and the wildness in a human being. Otherwise I'm not interested. So, when I meet people in reality, or in dreams, there's always a kind of animal awake in the person. Not necessarily horses. But the aptitude or the capacity for metamorphosis. Exactly as somebody can be metamorphosed into a devil or an angel, or a stone (you see people turning to stone), they can also, most of the time, turn to animals. Which is not a bad thing, on the contrary...

IAN BLYTH
University of St. Andrews

NOTES

1. The following interview took place during Hélène Cixous's visit to St Andrews University on June 24, 1999. I would first of all like to thank Hélène Cixous for agreeing to do the interview and for her help afterwards in composing the transcript. I would also like to thank Susan Sellers for, amongst other things, making the interview possible, and Gill Plain, who read through an early draft of this paper.
2. Hélène Cixous and Mireille Calle-Gruber, 'We Are Already in the Jaws of the Book: Inter Views', in Hélène Cixous and Mireille Calle-Gruber, *Hélène Cixous Rootprints: Memory and Life Writing*, translated by Eric Prenowitz (London, Routledge, 1997), pp. 3-115 (p. 84).
3. Hélène Cixous, *Three Steps on the Ladder of Writing*, translated by Sarah Cornell and Susan Sellers (New York, Columbia University Press, 1993), p. 38.
4. Hélène Cixous, *FirstDays of the Year*, translated by Catherine A. F. MacGillivray (Minneapolis, University of Minnesota Press, 1998), p. 11.
5. Hélène Cixous, 'Writing Blind: Conversation with the Donkey', translated by Eric Prenowitz, in Hélène Cixous, *Stigmata: Escaping Texts* (London, Routledge, 1998), p. 146.
6. Hélène Cixous, *Readings: The Poetics of Blanchot, Joyce, Kafka, Kleist, Lispector, and Tsvetayeva*, edited and translated by Verena Andermatt Conley (Minneapolis, University of Minnesota Press, 1991), p. 44; Hélène Cixous, *Reading with Clarice Lispector*, edited and translated by Verena Andermatt Conley (Minneapolis, University of Minnesota Press, 1990), p. 41.
7. Hélène Cixous, 'Inter Views', p. 28.

Hélène Cixous, *Tambours sur la digue*, performed by the Théâtre du Soleil, Paris, May 2000: A First Response

Cixous's most recent play *Tambours sur la digue* (*Drums Beating on the Dyke*), performed by the Théâtre du Soleil has met with widespread public and critical acclaim in France.[1] Indeed, the play won awards for best set, best director and best dramatic creation at this year's 'Molières', but the company caused a stir by refusing to attend the awards' ceremony, accusing the television companies of glamorizing 'theatre people' while remaining hostile to the broadcasting of plays. The praise for *Tambours sur la digue* forms a stark contrast to the adverse critical response afforded *Et soudain les nuits d'eveil* (*And Suddenly (on) nights of awakening*), another recent play which alternated with it during its run at the Cartoucherie. The latter, which marked a return to the company's original practice of collective collaboration, whilst reaping much praise from general audiences, was accused in many reviews of adopting a simplistic and reductive political stance in relation to both the situation of immigrants whose legal status has been affected by changes in French law, and the struggle for independence in Tibet.

Tambours sur la digue is an exhilarating and thought-provoking three-hour piece which builds both on the Théâtre du Soleil's continuing interest in non-western theatre, here specifically the Japanese traditions of Noh and Bunraku, and on Cixous's interest in the figure of the marionette that originates in her work on Kleist.[2] The play takes place in an ancient but unnamed Eastern realm and presents the dilemmas, corruption and betrayals of a regime forced to sacrifice a region, with its inhabitants, in the face of a flood of catastrophic proportions which threatens to breach all defences. Here, the city is privileged over the countryside, vested interests of an elite over the rural population, who are to be sacrificed in a plan to weaken one of the dykes deliberately in order to relieve pressure on the other. The political machinations, greed and ultimate incompetence of the builders of both regime and dyke are contrasted with a group of heroic but powerless figures: the Divine and his daughter, Madame Li the noodle seller, the sentries who watch over the kingdom and an old puppeteer. The final scenes are witness to a relentless chain of ambushes, murders and revenge killings, yet the flood is not averted.

The subtitle of *Tambours sur la digue* is 'an ancient play for marionettes performed by actors', yet this does not fully account for the complex dynamics represented on stage and maintained between actor, controller and spectator. Each character is presented as a puppet – the actors' stylized movements, gestures and lack of facial expression (their features both hidden and emphasized by layers of tights and make-up) replicating that of puppets. Each puppet, each character, has its puppeteer (*manipulateur*) dressed in the traditional black costume and veil of the Bunraku 'controller'[3] who accompanies the puppet throughout, originating their movements and ensuring their entry and exit from the stage. Unlike the Bunraku plays, whose dialogue is chanted by one narrator, these puppets, however, have kept their voices. The relationship between controller and puppet is both sinister and moving: the former's rapt attentiveness to the puppet's every movement and the proximity of both body and gaze is striking, yet the puppet's lack of reciprocal gaze emphasizes the power relation and thus highlights the central fascinating tension at work here between the apparent lack of subjectivity of the puppets and their ability to engage the audience entirely in their fates.

The theoretical implications of the status of these puppet/actors is clearly central to both Cixous's text and Mnouchkine's production. In an essay which accompanies the published text of the play, Cixous explains how she employs the structure of the relationship between puppet and puppeteer to reflect upon the processes both of writing and acting. Although tempted by the image of the puppet as an ideal state for the writer of theatre (herself as the puppet, the strings of her imagination pulled by the Chinese poet His-Xhou), she acknowledges that this vision of the author as moved, mute receptacle of an ancient inspiration retains the status of a dream rather than the lived reality of writing, a reality which remains governed by the author's cultural heritage and theatrical tradition.[4] This use of the puppet trope is extended to Cixous's discussion of the relationship between actor and director, not in order to designate a simple hierarchy of controller and controlled but to describe the work of the actor as both puppeteer and puppet,[5] a doubling which is likened to the process of writing.[6] This leads in turn to a more general reflection on the structure of social identities, proposing them as conscious and manipulated versions of our inner selves with which we superficially identify, but which act as shields and disguises to our more fragile pluralities:

La marionnette est l'extériorisation de la marionnettiste intérieure que nous sommes. Intérieurement nous sommes des êtres démultipliés, compliqués, articulés. Les personnes sociales que nous nous obligeons d'être sont des simplifications identificatoires et illisibles, des ecrans opaques, des boucliers. ('Le Théâtre surpris par les marionnettes', 119)

(The puppet is the exteriorization of the interior puppeteer that we are. On the inside we are multiple, complicated, spoken/structured. The social beings that we force ourselves to be are identificatory [for the purposes of identifying with others] and illegible simplifications, opaque screens, shields.)

Such theoretical investment in the metaphors of the puppet does not however diminish the fascinating presence of these puppet-subjects on the stage, these figures whose scale and voices are wholly human, but whose movements and expressions remain those of manipulated objects. Human puppets are perhaps the most fitting characters for a narrative which condemns the abuse of power and the helplessness of humanity in the face of the forces of both nature and corrupt government, yet the beauty of their gestures and the impassivity of their faces arguably draw the audience's attention away from the verbal and narrative elements of the performance.

Two central, sensual aspects of the play work against abstract metaphors of alterity to immerse the audience in the action and setting of the play. First, the complex relationship I have pointed to between actors, puppets, controllers and spectators is offset by the visual simplicity of the set which is both minimalist and sumptuous, evoking an abstract Japanese landscape with its wooden decking, pebbles and immense silk backdrops of skyscapes whose dramatic falls to the floor (they change twenty-two times) punctuate the play. The central area is bordered by narrow canals of water into which each character dips their hand at some point in the play – the water which is both life force and agent of diluvial disaster serves to quench thirsts, reflect anguish and wash away blood.[7] The collapse of the stage floor to reveal a pit of flood water in the final scene provides a shocking emphasis on the human scale of such tragedies. Second, the drums of the play's title disrupt the dominant tone of the play and perform a similar function to that of Kyogen drama which provides contrasting comic interludes in productions of Noh theatre. Here, the precision and apparent fragility of the puppet's movements is offset in the final scene before the interval by an incredible rhythmic assault on the senses. Duan, the Divine's daughter, journeys to the mountains overlooking the city and the dyke to prepare the sentries for the possible need to alert the

Hélène Cixous, Tambours sur la digue, *performed by the Théâtre du Soleil* 347

population to danger of flooding. Such warnings are given by the beating of drums, and the scene climaxes with thirty drummers rehearsing messages of alarm and confidence whilst their controllers hang from the rafters of the building apparently straining to control their movements. The sonic shock of the drums' rhythm and volume coupled with the visual impact of the exuberant choreography of their movements provides a welcome release of tension and freedom of movement at the end of the first part of the play.

The denouement of *Tambours sur la digue* merits particular attention. In the final scene, following the murder or disappearance of all of the main characters in turn, the stage falls eerily silent as puppets, the wooden objects belonging to the aged puppeteer, are flung into the newly-revealed pit of water in the centre of the stage. The puppeteer, at first alone, and then joined by the controllers, solemnly recovers the figures and positions them on the front ledge of the stage, facing the audience. The impact of the silence in contrast to Lemêtre's hitherto constant musical accompaniment, the sound of rushing silk and water, and the surprise to the spectator at the diminutive scale of the puppets is immense and increases as the audience gradually realizes that the puppets are indeed miniatures of the characters of the play. The effect brings to mind Anthony Gormley's artwork 'Field for the British Isles' in which gallery floors were filled with 35,000 roughly hewn, diminutive clay figures whose beseeching gaze seemed to implore the spectator to empathy, to action and, paradoxically, to a recognition of a common humanity.[8] The scene also recalls the silent scene in Cixous's own *La Ville parjure ou le reveil des Erinyes* (*The Perjured City or the Awakening of the Erinyes*) when the mother is visited by the spirits of her dead children,[9] yet I would argue that the impact here is greater due to the abrupt change in scale of the figures and the complex relationships built up between spectator and puppet over the course of the play. The audience has been fascinated by the life-size puppets and their controllers, marvelling at the technical skill of the actors and the ingenuity of the direction, and accepting these figures as puppets. The final scene represents more than an overworked *mise en abyme* of the narrative as it changes the emotional tone of the piece entirely.[10] The vision of the wooden figures dear to the old puppeteer, lying helpless and immobile in the water, with no means of interacting with an environment which is both out of their control and out of their scale, constitutes an explicit invitation to the audience to establish their own position between controller and puppet, both in relation to the ethical questions broached in the play, and in terms of their own responsibility, agency and identities.

Since her epic dramas of the 1980s, Cixous's plays have employed elements of classical myth, legend and recent history to assert the scale of tragedy of contemporary events without engaging in a direct portrayal of them. This powerful play continues this aspect of her work and functions as a fable designed to reflect indirectly on contemporary tragedy (here the creative catalyst was the recent floods in China)[11] and its wider metaphorical interpretations, the presence of the puppet-subjects confronting the audience with more general questions of the abuse of power and manipulation. Yet the play also clearly articulates its engagement with another of Cixous's and Mnouchkine's established concerns, that of the role and nature of theatre itself. Jean-Louis Perrier remarks on this aspect of the final scene, describing it as: 'une conclusion admirable, où, peut-être, se conjuguent le salut au public et le salut tout court, l'éphémère du théâtre et sa renaissance éternelle'[12] (an admirable conclusion, in which perhaps we see combined the salute to the audience and salvation itself, the ephemeral nature of the theatre and its eternal renaissance). The old puppeteer is the sole character to survive the flood in his role as creator, actor and perhaps personification of the art of theatre. Through his positioning of the puppets and their ambiguous state (are they simply salvage or survivors?), he confronts the audience with both our complicity in the tragedies of the past and our potential agency in imagining new beginnings.

JULIA DOBSON
University of Wolverhampton

NOTES

1 The play was in production at the Cartoucherie from September 1999 to June 2000.
2 See, for example, Hélène Cixous, *Readings. The Poetics of Blanchot, Joyce, Kafka, Kleist, Lispector and Tsvetayeva*, translated by Verena Andermatt Conley, (New York and London, Harvester Wheatsheaf, 1992).
3 Bunraku developed a system of three controllers per puppet: one controlled the feet, one the left hand and one the right hand and head.
4 Hélène Cixous, 'Le Théâtre surpris par les marionnettes', in *Tambours sur la digue* (Paris, Théâtre du Soleil, 1999), pp. 115-124 (p. 116).
5 'Le metteur en scène demande à l'acteur d'être deux. Ne va pas plus vite que ce que tu peux faire en étant deux' ('Le Théâtre surpris par les marionnettes', p. 118) (The director asks the actor to be two. Go no faster than you can whilst being two people).

6   'Sois deux, c'est l'écriture même. La marionnette écrit avec des temps, des intervalles nets, des blancs (invisibles)' ('Le Théâtre surpris par les marionnettes', p. 121) (Be two: it's writing itself. The puppet writes with time, with precise intervals, blanks (which are invisible)).

7   The image of the river as narrative and as representative of the stream of human tragedy has been employed before by Cixous. See, for example, the programme notes to *La Ville parjure ou le reveil des Erinyes.*

8   This artwork, which toured the U.K in 1994-5, remains one of the most prominent works of the 1990s and has been widely written about. For illustrations, essays and Gormley's own views on the piece see Anthony Gormley, *Field for the British Isles* (Llandudno, Oriel Mostyn, 1994).

9   Hélène Cixous, *La Ville parjure ou le reveil des Erinyes* (Paris, Théâtre du soleil, 1994).

10 Cixous refers to this in her essay that accompanies the published text of the play: 'Soudain nous sentons à pleurer que c'est nous: quand la figure est si éternelle et le corps si fragile qu'il ne peut pas se crisper sans se briser, c'est nous, le créature humaine environnée par les vents du temps, miniscule dans l'Histoire des Forces et des Pouvoirs' ('Le Théâtre surpris par les marionnettes', pp. 120-1) (Suddenly we are moved to tears by the recognition that this is us: when the face is so timeless and the body so fragile that it cannot tense without breaking, it is us, the human race, blown by the winds of time, minuscule in the History of Forces and Powers).

11 See interview with Ariane Mnouchkine at www.lcr-rouge.org.fr .

12 Jean-Louis Perrier, *Le Monde* (September 25th 1999), 21.

Hélène Cixous – Selected Bibliography

Books in French

Place of publication is Paris, unless otherwise indicated.

Prénom de Dieu, short stories, Grasset, 1967
L'Exil de Joyce ou l'art du remplacement, doctoral thesis, Grasset, 1968
Dedans, novel (*Prix Médicis*), Grasset, 1969 (re-published, des femmes, 1986)
Le Troisième Corps, novel, Grasset, 1970 (re-published, des femmes, 1999)
Les Commencements, novel, Grasset, 1970 (re-published, des femmes, 1999)
Un vrai jardin, poetic short story, L'Herne, 1971 (re-published, des femmes, 1998)
Neutre, novel, Grasset, 1972 (re-published, des femmes, 1998)
Tombe, novel, Seuil, 1973
Portrait du soleil, novel, Denoël, 1973 (re-published, des femmes, 1999)
Prénoms de personne, 'poetic' collection, Seuil, 1974
Révolution pour plus d'un Faust, novel, Seuil, 1975
Souffles, fiction, des femmes, 1975 (new edition, 1998)
La Jeune Née, essay (with Catherine Clément), 10/18, 1975
Un K. incompréhensible: Pierre Goldman, essay, Christian Bourgois, 1975
Portrait de Dora, theatre, des femmes, 1976
La, fiction, Gallimard, 1976 (re-published, des femmes, 1979)
Angst, fiction, des femmes, 1977 (new edition, 1998)
Preparatifs de noces, fiction, des femmes, 1978 (on cassette, read by the author, 1981)
Le Nom d'Oedipe, theatre, des femmes, 1978
La Pupille, theatre, Cahiers Renaud-Barrault, 1978
Partie, fiction, des femmes, 1979
Ananke, fiction, des femmes, 1979
Vivre l'orange, fiction, des femmes, 1979
Illa, fiction, des femmes, 1980
With ou l'art de l'innocence, fiction, des femmes, 1981
Limonade tout était si infini, fiction, des femmes, 1982

Le Livre de Promethea, fiction, Gallimard, 1983
L'Histoire terrible mais inachevée de Norodom Sihanouk, roi du Cambodge, theatre, Théâtre du Soleil, 1985
La Prise de l'école de Madhubaï, theatre, des femmes, 1986
Théâtre, theatre, des femmes, 1986
Entre l'écriture, essay, des femmes, 1986
La Bataille d'Arcachon, Trois (Québec), 1986
L'Indiade, ou l'Inde de leurs rêves, theatre, Théâtre du Soleil, 1987
Manne aux Mandelstams aux Mandelas, fiction, des femmes, 1988
L'Heure de Clarice Lispector, preceded by *Vivre l'orange*, fiction, des femmes, 1989
Jours de l'an, fiction, des femmes, 1990
L'Ange au secret, fiction, des femmes, 1991
Déluge, fiction, des femmes, 1992
On ne part pas, on ne revient pas, theatre, des femmes, 1992 (on cassette, read by Nicole Garcia, Daniel Mesguich, Christèle Wurmser, Bernard Yerlès, 1992)
Beethoven à jamais ou l'existence de Dieu, fiction, des femmes, 1993
L'Histoire (qu'on ne connaîtra jamais), theatre, des femmes, 1994
La Ville parjure ou le reveil des Erinyes, theatre, Théâtre du Soleil, 1994
Hélène Cixous, Photos de racines, essay with Mireille Calle-Gruber, des femmes, 1994
La Fiancée juive de la tentation, fiction, des femmes, 1995
Messie, fiction, des femmes, 1996
OR, les lettres de mon père, fiction, des femmes, 1997
Voiles (with Jacques Derrida), Galilée, 1998
Osnabrück, novel, des femmes, 1999
Tambours sur la digue, theatre, Théâtre du Soleil, 1999
Les Rêveries de la femme sauvage: scènes primitives, Galilée, 2000

Books Available in English Translation

The Exile of James Joyce, translated by Sally Purcell (New York, David Lewis & London, John Calder, 1976; New York, Riverrun, 1980)
Portrait of Dora, translated by Anita Barrows (London, John Calder, 1979)
Angst, translated by Jo Levy (London, John Calder, 1985)
Inside, translated by Carol Barko (New York, Shocken Books, 1986)
The Newly Born Woman, translated by Betsy Wing (Minneapolis, Minnesota University Press, 1986; republished London, I.B. Tauris, 1996)

Reading with Clarice Lispector, edited and translated by Verena Andermatt Conley (Minneapolis, Minnesota University Press & Hemel Hempstead, Harvester Wheatsheaf, 1990)

The Book of Promethea, translated by Betsy Wing (Lincoln, University of Nebraska Press, 1991)

'Coming to Writing' and Other Essays, translated by Sarah Cornell, Deborah Jensen, Ann Liddle and Susan Sellers (Cambridge, Mass., and London, Harvard University Press, 1991)

Readings: The Poetics of Blanchot, Joyce, Kafka, Kleist, Lispector and Tsvetayeva, translated by Verena Andermatt Conley (Hemel Hempstead, Harvester Wheatsheaf, 1992)

Three Steps on the Ladder of Writing, translated by Sarah Cornell and Susan Sellers (New York, Columbia University Press, 1993)

The Hélène Cixous Reader, edited by Susan Sellers (London, Routledge, 1994)

Manna for the Mandelstams for the Mandelas, translated by Catherine A.F. MacGillivray (Minneapolis, University of Minnesota, 1994)

The Terrible but Unfinished Story of Norodom Sihanouk, King of Cambodia, translated by Lollie Groth and Judith Pike (Lincoln, University of Nebraska Press, 1994)

Hélène Cixous, Rootprints: Memory and Life Writing, with Mireille Calle-Gruber, translated by Keith Cohen, Catherine A.F. MacGillivray and Eric Prenowitz (London and New York, Routledge, 1997)

Stigmata, Escaping Texts (London and New York, Routledge, 1998)

FirstDays of the Year, translated by Catherine A.F. MacGillivray (Minneapolis and London, University of Minnesota Press, 1998)